Wicked TERRE HAUTE

Tim Crumrin

Published by The History Press
Charleston, SC
www.historypress.net

Copyright © 2019 by Tim Crumrin
All rights reserved

First published 2019

Manufactured in the United States

ISBN 9781467140744

Library of Congress Control Number: 2018963528

Notice: The information in this book is true and complete to the best of our knowledge. It is offered without guarantee on the part of the author or The History Press. The author and The History Press disclaim all liability in connection with the use of this book.

All rights reserved. No part of this book may be reproduced or transmitted in any form whatsoever without prior written permission from the publisher except in the case of brief quotations embodied in critical articles and reviews.

*Dedicated to Steve Cox, Ph.D.
Mentor, colleague, great friend, kindred spirit*

CONTENTS

Acknowledgements	7
Introduction	9
FRAIL SISTERHOOD OF THE BAGNIO	**11**
Sex Tourism	14
Bagnio Scenes	15
A House Can Be a Home	19
The Death of Coal Oil Johnny	21
Girls Will Be Girls	24
The First Madam Brown	26
The Gathering	28
CURSE OF THE WHITE QUEEN OF CHINATOWN	**30**
THE OTHER WEST END	**36**
People of the Dump	37
DUH MAYOR	**41**
KING OF THE VICE TRUST	**46**
The Case of the Missing Slot Machines	50
THE QUEEN AND CROWN PRINCE OF VICE	**56**

Contents

A Gangster Named Boobie	**65**
Our Gangs	**73**
A Hautean Rogues' Gallery	75
Fast Women, Faster Cars	78
Life as a Gamble	78
Up the Road	84
The Liquor Ring	86
Blood on the Streets	**89**
Gang Wars	90
Thousands Die	95
Good Cop, Bad Cop	**97**
Red Light, Red Light	**103**
The Reverend Mr. Keen	104
The Business of Prostitution	107
The Golden Age	109
A Madam's Life	**111**
Staff Training	112
Tricks of the Trade	112
Love	114
A Day in the Life	116
Caste System	117
From Terre Haute to Eternity	**118**
Any Publicity Is Good Publicity?	**122**
And Sin No More	**128**
Epilogue	135
Bibliography	137
About the Author	143

ACKNOWLEDGEMENTS

Anyone researching the history of Terre Haute owes a huge debt of gratitude to Mike McCormick, the official Vigo County historian. Mike's depth and breadth of knowledge of Terre Haute is unequaled. I owe you, Mike. Terre Haute is lucky to have many institutions dedicated to preserving its history. Three were particularly helpful in researching this book. As always, Marylee Hagen, Susan Tingley and Rachel Wasmer of the Vigo County Historical Society offered their ever-smiling expertise. The staff at the Vigo County Public Library, including Matt Bird, JJ Coppinger, Janice Knight and Sean Eisele, remain indispensable sources for local history. Cinda May and Katie Sutrina-Haney of the Cunningham Memorial Library's Special Collections and University Archives at Indiana State University were helpful as always. My thanks to Bob Ferguson and Fred Nation, Cheryl Blevins and John Moats for sharing their insights and memories.

And, as always, to my wife, Robin, without whom…

INTRODUCTION

For over a century, Terre Haute, Indiana, was known as a "sin city." Its West End was one of the most notorious red-light districts in the Midwest. At its height, in the 1920s, it contained sixty brothels and nearly one thousand prostitutes. The city was also a haven for gamblers of all stripes, and in 1956, more bets were placed through a "wire room" in Terre Haute than anywhere in the nation except Las Vegas.

During Prohibition, it was a bootlegging center. With the illegal booze operations came gangsters and gang warfare. Hijackings, violence and murder were common as rival gangs from St. Louis and Chicago fought for turf.

This book tells the stories of the colorful people and events that gave Terre Haute its well-earned national reputation.

FRAIL SISTERHOOD OF THE BAGNIO

Prostitution is the so-called world's oldest profession. That designation may be debated, but it is a business that has always been part of society. It is perhaps, the profession whose "business plan" has changed the least over the millennia. It is now, as it ever was, a person (most often a woman) selling or bartering their body.

Over the years, prostitutes and their places of business have gone by many names: Cyprian, whore, lady of the night, streetwalker, tom, snapper, courtesan. The magnitude and variety of these terms helps to demonstrate the ubiquity of prostitution.

Terre Haute was founded in 1816. It was an overwhelmingly male place for its first decade or so. Gambling and drinking were likely the first vices. After all, those are things men did when they were in each other's company in frontier areas like early Terre Haute. By the early 1820s, Terre Haute had several inns that catered to townsmen and transients alike.

We do not know the name of the first prostitute to arrive in Terre Haute, nor the date of her arrival. But came they did. Besides welcoming travelers and locals, Terre Haute was often home to riverboat men and workers on the National Road, which became the town's main street. Later, it served as a base for canal workers and the navvies who built the railroads. These men were eager for a drink, a bet and the pleasure of a woman's company. There were even prostitutes who attached themselves to the construction crews, traveling with them like camp followers in the Civil War.

An Ordinance
For the Suppression of Vice and Immorality.
SEC. 1. Be it ordained by the Common Council of the Town of Terre-Haute, That all houses of ill-fame, all houses of assignation, and all assemblages at such houses either by night or by day, whereby the peace and quiet of neighborhoods and families are disturbed, and the moral sense of community is outraged; are hereby declared to be *Nuisances*, and as such subject to be removed, and that the keeper or keepers of such house or houses, shall be subject to a penalty of ten dollars, to be recovered by suit before the Mayor, together with costs of prosecution, for every day such nuisances are continued.

Sec. 2. *Be it further ordained*, That no person or persons residing in the town of Terre-Haute, shall knowingly, harbor or keep about his, her, or their premises in said town, any lewd baudy or dissolute woman, who, while thus residing with said person, obtains her living by prostitution, under a penalty of five dollars for every day such woman is so kept, to be recovered with costs of suit as aforesaid.

Sec. 3. *Be it further ordained*, That no person shall rent, lease, or hire any house, room or other building to be used as a disorderly or baudy house within said town; and if any person having leased or rented any house, room or other building in said town professedly for a lawful purpose, and shall afterwards during the continuance of said lease, use the same for the purpose of keeping such disorderly or baudy house, or shall suffer the same to be so used, such illegal use or occupancy of such house, room or other building, shall be a forfeiture of the lease by which said house, room or building shall be holden; and the landlord of such tenant knowing of such illegal use of such house, room or other building, who shall fail to re-enter upon such premises and abate such nuisance, shall be proceeded against and be liable to the same penalties, as the keeper or keepers of such disorderly or baudy house, room or other building.

Approved, August 8, 1842.
D. S. DANALDSON, President.
Attest: W. M. MODESITT, Clerk.
August 27–51–13

The 1842 Terre Haute ordinance that made prostitution illegal. *Vigo County Historical Society.*

Initially, prostitution was likely conducted by a woman working alone or perhaps two women who banded together. They would meet men in saloons or inns. Their assignations would take place in an inn room, the back of a saloon or any other spot that was available. That spot might be an alley, a stable or in a convenient bush. It was hardly glamorous.

Eventually, they gathered together in a single location such as a house or the second floor of a saloon or other building. The first of the brothels that would so be associated with Terre Haute was formed by 1840.

Prostitution became so well ensconced in Terre Haute by the 1850s that brothels (*bagnio*, derived from the Italian word for public bath, was the oft-used nineteenth-century term) sprouted along the town's rutted streets. They became such a problem that the common council had to enact an ordinance against them in 1842: "That all houses of ill fame, houses of assignation…be classified as *nuisances*, and as such are subject to be removed."

The first woman to be publicly named as a madam was Sue Garvin in 1867. She was arrested along with two of her "girls." One of the girls was Charlotte Hammonds, who later opened her own bagnio and became quite notorious. Appropriately enough, her house was at Third and Cherry Streets, which was within an area along the Wabash River later "designated" by local authorities as the boundaries of the red-light district. She was not the last madam to rise to notoriety. Unlike later Terre Haute newspapers, nineteenth-century papers delighted in stories of madams and their girls. The stories were presented with a mix of bemusement and horror at the dissolution acted out upon the streets of Terre Haute on a daily basis.

Though many of the brothels were located in the West End, they seeped into other parts of town following the Civil War. It would not be until the turn of the century that the West End once again held the majority of bagnios within its scandalous environs.

The bagnios varied greatly—some were clean and well-ordered, while others were literally disorderly houses. Perhaps the absolute worst was just across the river bridge near the Terre Haute city limits, which butted up against the miasmic bottomlands of the Wabash in a dismal, disease-infested area later known as Taylorville. Amid hovels that were little more than lean-tos was a grimy, crime-ridden little tent city. Some of the tents were little more than portable bagnios. One was the domain of an unwashed, haggard "river bottom prostitute." She was surrounded by sickly-looking, half-clad women. These places were lowliest of the low, where a woman's body could be bought for as little as a dime or a half-eaten loaf of bread. It was degradation at its worst.

Judging from the list of names of madams, it is safe to estimate that there were at least twenty-five or more brothels in Terre Haute at any given time in the last quarter of the nineteenth century.

Of course, not all Terre Haute prostitutes worked in brothels. There were also streetwalkers who were known as wandering prostitutes. They indeed walked the streets of residential areas, tempting husbands with wandering eyes, inexperienced young boys or whoever strolled by. Ida Jones and Mattie Gray were arrested for trolling in neighborhoods on the same night in 1867. Evidently, business was not good that evening, as both were listed as impecunious and unable to pay fines of $8.95 and were sent to jail. In 1880, a woman named Mary Meyers was arrested and fined $7.70. The man who was caught with her was William Graham, who was fined $9.70 for associating with a prostitute. As they were "caught," it is likely they were enjoying each other in a public place. Sometimes they had to use alleyways, clumps of trees or darkened streets.

Some wandering girls had houses (perhaps their own homes) or had access to houses of assignation. These were the no-tell motels of the day. These might have been hotels that rented rooms by the hour or, in some cases, people would rent a room in their home or apartment for the assignation of a prostitute and her customer.

The Meyers-Graham case illustrated several important aspects of nineteenth-century prostitution. The "sentence" for prostitution was a fine, not imprisonment. It was not until the 1970s that prostitution became a crime that entailed jail time. And the names of "johns" were published in local newspapers along with those of prostitutes. Association with prostitutes was against the law, and men usually were given a larger fine.

Sex Tourism

Terre Haute's reputation made it a place for the sex tourist. Since the city also offered a range of gambling dens and saloons everywhere you looked, it was rather like a Las Vegas of its day. What happened in Terre Haute stayed in Terre Haute, usually. Men came from all over western Indiana and eastern Illinois to indulge in the delights of a sin city without the chance of being caught by folks back home.

Such was the case of the "Decatur Boobies."

A newspaper headlined the story "Couple Sucker Toughs Came to Grief" in the West End. "Sucker" was an early nickname for people from Illinois. It seems a baker named Dale and a machinist named Hallard decided to lead a group of "would be toughs" from Decatur to Terre Haute for a good time one Saturday in 1891. After visiting a bagnio, they filled their guts with whiskey and beer. They then decided it might be fun to start bowling empty beer kegs down the street. That was so much fun that when the scamps spied a broken telephone pole, they rolled it down the street to block a driveway.

A policeman happened upon the scene and spoiled their fun by making them clean up their mess. Later, the same cop was investigating a quarrel in a bagnio when what did he find but the boys from Decatur. They were whooping and hollering up and down the street and generally having a good old time despite the earlier warning to behave. The officer grabbed the "loudest and smartest" of the revelers. When they allowed as to how they did not feel like going back to the jail with him, he banged their hard heads together and marched them off. To avoid a Sunday in jail, they offered their watches as their bond. They then hotfooted it to the depot and grabbed the next train to Decatur, forfeiting their bond.

The next day, their watches went up for sale at the jail.

A visit to a brothel was clearly a rite of passage for many young men. In their constantly fevered minds, the bagnio was a scented repository of their hardiest dreams, a place of untold delights where secrets of another world would be revealed to them. There were instances of fathers taking their young sons there to introduce them to the mysteries of life. But more often, it was a more experienced friend escorting a shy young man for the "experience of his life."

A scene that played out in tiny Union City, Indiana, also took place many times in Terre Haute. A teenage lothario named Meier resolved to take his shy friend to the local bagnio. At first, his friend was almost quivering with excitement, but that changed to hesitation as they entered the door. Several women walked into the parlor to display themselves for selection. One of them saw that the shy boy was very jittery and looked unsure of himself. "One girl raised her dress up above her head," revealing things the shy boy had never seen. He grabbed his friend and launched himself out of the house, not slowing until he was well on the road back to the farm.

Some brothels listed themselves as laundries and the prostitutes as laundresses. This helped to cover their activities and explain the stream of men coming to their doors at all hours. This also gave cover to the johns, who could say they were merely taking in their soiled clothes to be washed. It is not difficult to imagine a young farmhand or laborer, with a wink and knowing smile, using the phrase "going to get my laundry done" among his friends as a slang term for his real actions.

The type of women working as prostitutes also greatly varied, though it appears they tended to be young, some as young as thirteen. There were older, more experienced women "on the game," but then as now, it was mainly a young woman's world. They became prostitutes for reasons as varied as themselves. Many were escaping abusive home lives, seeking adventure or making more money than they would in another profession such as teaching.

The economics of prostitution were much the same as in later years. Typically, it was a fifty-fifty split between the prostitute and the madam. The madam also dunned the girls for their room and board and other expenses, so they ultimately might keep only about half of their original share. Some madams took this very seriously. Madam Hammond, a notorious Terre Haute figure, sued one of the girls who left her employ for a thirteen-dollar boarding bill. The judge ruled for the young woman and added insult to injury by making the madam pay five dollars in court costs.

It is likely that most Terre Haute bagnios of the period were dollar houses. It cost a man around one dollar for his short time with a woman. Undoubtedly, some charged more, but many others only charged fifty cents. It was a tough way to make a living.

BAGNIO SCENES

Sometimes love bloomed in a bagnio, and one time it took place between May and December. John Strain, a sixty-year-old wealthy farmer, married young Lizzie Bingham. He had been "visiting" her at the bagnio for some time. Indeed, he had been arrested and fined several times for "associating with a prostitute." He happily took his new wife back to the farm and away from her old life. How seriously Lizzie took to farm life versus bagnio life is unknown.

In 1883, John Callahan married Betty Landry, aka Cora Lee, a bagnio keeper. Judging from later reports, she ignored her wedding vows and continued in her business.

Some women became prostitutes because they thought there was a certain glamour to the profession. They imagined pretty clothes, jewelry, an exciting life and more money than they could ever make as a housemaid. But for some, it was a life that wore on them. Taking to bed men of all sorts—drunk, smelly, rough—could dispirit many. Their hoped-for glamorous life turned into a soul-sapping degraded existence. The situation became so desperate for some they could only see one way out.

Two young women fell into the abyss on a dreary February day in 1883. Ada Ray, a young woman from Crawfordsville, moved to Terre Haute to join her sister at Madam Jaycox's bagnio. Neither sister found the exciting life they hoped for. Unhappy at the Jaycox place, they left to ply their trade at several other brothels in town. They found life no more golden there and eventually returned to the Jaycox house.

After another night of being pushed, pulled, grabbed and probed by strange men, Ada woke up to a dark morning. She looked around her, looked out the window and looked at her rapidly aging face in the mirror. In none of those places did she see a happy future. From a hiding spot in her room, she took out a small glass bottle. In the bottle was a poison called Paris Green. With trembling hands, she put it to her lips, closed her eyes and drank it.

When Ada's sister awoke, she saw that Ada seemed to be in a haze. Ada weakly announced she was tired of living, that death seemed to be the answer to her troubles. Her sister hurriedly roused Madam Jaycox, who sent for a doctor. The doctor, having seen such scenes too often, arrived and gave Ada an emetic. Her body soon expelled the poison. He advised rest for Ada to let her get back her strength.

Three days later, Ada was once again in the Jaycox parlor waiting for a man to choose her.

The same day as Ada's suicide attempt, another young prostitute walked down the same path but for different reasons. Laura Pollock worked at Sallie Miller's bagnio. Laura, nicknamed "Silver Heel" for some reason, had fallen in love with another West End character, Dick Kinman, a bartender at one of the many saloons there who had acquired the unenviable nickname of "Stink Foot."

But the course of the romance of Silver Heel and Stink Foot did not run smoothly. Stink Foot had a wandering eye. Laura learned that her beloved had taken up with a "handsomer girl." Feeling she had lost out to her prettier rival and all hope was gone, Laura took an overdose of morphine. Whether she did this to end it all or perhaps was thinking the gesture would convince Stink Foot of her undying love is unknown. Again, a doctor was summoned and emetics administered. Like Ada, Laura returned to the bagnio.

When there exists a group of young women vying for the attention of any man who walked into the bagnio, there is bound to be a certain tension and jealousy.

On a Sunday night in August 1883, the newly installed telephone at police headquarters jangled, and an excited voice yelled down the line that all hell had broken loose at the Michaels's bagnio on North Fourth Street. Two policeman jumped in the paddy wagon and sped to the scene. By the time they arrived, they found an air of false calm among the ladies gathered in the parlor. All sat about in various stages of undress as if nothing was amiss. It was not until later that the truth was revealed.

It seemed that the madam had recently added a young woman of particular beauty to her inventory. The lovely newcomer was of the haughty sort and was much hated by the others. After all, she was much in demand by the clients and was taking money out of her colleagues' pockets. The fetid air of the muggy night had everyone on edge. So, emboldened by drink, one of her rivals decided that she'd had about all she could take of her conceited rival. A drink was thrown, and the fight was on. It was described as a catfight to end all catfights. A flurry of hair-pulling, scratching, biting, kicking and cursing filled the bagnio. When no one else stepped in to stop the fight (why should they, as their friend was doing exactly what they all wished to do), the madam rushed in and managed to separate the disheveled combatants. She sent them out into the steamy night, in opposite directions, to cool off.

They were absent when the police arrived, so the officers climbed back in the wagon wondering if the telephone would be ringing again soon.

Though some families swallowed their pride and took the money sent to them by their prostitute daughter or sister, for most, the descent into the bagnio was viewed with a mixture of shame and horror. It was not a life most families ever envisioned for a little girl as she was growing up.

On Saturday, February 11, 1883 sixteen-year-old Mayme Call was arrested for prostitution. The next morning, she was released from the Terre

Haute jail and immediately went to Casto's drugstore on Main Street. She nervously went to the counter and ordered a fifteen-cent bottle of morphine. She went upstairs and swallowed the full contents. When her suicide was discovered, she was taken to her mother's house, where she had been arrested the previous night.

Three days later, an old man from Cory, Indiana, arrived in Terre Haute to collect his Civil War pension. He was still working at a flour mill in Coal City, but his pension was certainly helpful. After getting his money, he decided to have lunch at a restaurant before heading home. He settled in his chair, and the proprietor came to take his order.

When his meal came, the café owner stayed to make conversation. He asked the stranger if he had heard about the terrible news that a young girl had killed herself. He told the old man the poor girl's name was Mayme, Mayme Call. The old man raised his head in shock. "I had a daughter by that name. I wonder if it could be her." The owner saw a tear form in the old man's eye and then etch its way down his cheek.

Later, the old man told his tale to a reporter. "For eighteen years, I lived with my wife and was happy." They had eight children, he told the reporter. "Mary, or Mayme, as she was called, was our youngest." But thirteen years earlier, his wife had deserted the family, taking Mayme with her. His wife had taken up with a tramp and left town with him. Not long afterward, her new man was convicted of a felony and sent to prison.

The old man believed his wife and Mayme had meandered into Terre Haute. His wife began working as a prostitute, probably in a small bagnio. It appeared that she eventually set up her own small brothel. Evidently, Mayme was forced to take up her mother's profession.

Mr. Call lost touch with them not long after his wife took up her new wayward life. The sad news of his daughter's death was the first he had heard of her in years. Call went to the address he was given, a small house on the West End. The first person he saw was his wayward wife. The years of hard living were traced on her face, but he immediately recognized her. She took him into a small bedroom, where he saw his daughter for the first time in thirteen years.

His mind reeled. All he could think was that it was such a hideous death for such a sweet girl. Still, he wondered if perhaps she was "better off dead than alive," considering the "circumstances and the curse of her wasted life falls upon her mother."

He buried Mayme at Highland Lawn Cemetery in Terre Haute and returned to Cory a "heartbroken old man."

Some fathers did all they could to "rescue" their daughters. In 1880, a farmer from Marshall, Illinois, arrived in Terre Haute looking for his daughter. He tracked down a policeman and asked for help finding his wayward child. The policeman took him on a round of the bagnios. They finally found her. At first, his daughter refused to go with him, saying she preferred her exciting new life to the backbreaking chores on the farm. But when she was told she would be dragged out kicking and screaming if needed, she reluctantly agreed to leave. The story she told was all too familiar to the policeman. She had been seduced by a saloon owner. He treated her like a queen—for a while. Then he pimped her out to a local madam and visited her several times a week.

The police in Terre Haute were actually very good at helping parents get their daughters back. And the kinder ones, who likely were fathers themselves, kept an eye out for newcomers, especially teenage girls. They removed them from bagnios and sent them home or turned them over to charity groups set up to rescue prostitutes.

Sometimes, a would-be damsel in distress refused to leave. A man from Brazil came to Terre Haute looking for his daughter. He knew the bagnio she was in, and the police went with him to get the girl, but she had been spirited away and was in hiding until her father left town.

Another young girl from Brazil liked her new life and was none too happy when police whisked her away from the house. As she had little clothing of her own, another girl in the bagnio loaned her a dress. The girl, named Ava, told the marshal taking her back to Brazil that as soon as she could get a dress and fifty cents for a train ticket, she was heading back to Terre Haute.

There was one attempted rescue that ended in tragedy. A young man named Bambo came from Paris to Terre Haute to look for his sister. The family was sure she had become a prostitute. He found her in a West End bagnio. He tried and tried to convince her to return home with him. When she obstinately told him that she was not about to return to Paris, her angry, frustrated brother pulled a gun and shot her. She finally returned to Paris, but not in the way her family had hoped.

A House Can Be a Home

The most famous madam in the United States was Polly Adler. Born in a Russian shtetl, she came to America seeking more than Russia could give her. By the mid-1920s, she was running one of the fanciest brothels in New

York City. It became the "in" thing for celebrities to visit her brothel. Since feared gangster Dutch Shultz was her friend and protector, she had little to fear from the authorities. In 1953, she wrote a book called *A House Is Not a Home* telling of her adventures in the skin trade.

But as the story of Mayme Call attests, whorehouses were also home to families. In modern times, fearless comedian Richard Pryor grew up in his grandmother's brothel in Peoria, Illinois. Prostitutes sometimes served as his babysitters.

Terre Haute had bagnios that were also family homes. A much scorned madam named Volger had her mother and daughter living with her in various bagnios around Terre Haute. One of the early madams in Terre Haute, Madam Hattie Jaycox, had a troublesome son living in her bagnio, much to the regret of her girls.

Clay Jaycox was a sullen lad who felt he could do anything he wanted in mom's house. In 1882, one of her prostitutes, Belle Buckingham, did something to anger Clay. He decided to show her just who was the boss by beating her up. A battered Belle was having none of that. She was not going to let the bastard get away with it, no matter who was his mother. She went to the police station and made a complaint. Six officers went to the bagnio and arrested Madam Jaycox and five of her prostitutes. Enraged by Belle's betrayal, Madam Jaycox posted bail for herself and the other five but left Belle in jail. Why Belle was also arrested is unknown, although it was likely because she was also one of the prostitutes. As for young Clay, he had slunk away and was in hiding.

In October 1886, two women stepped off the train from Crawfordsville and immediately drew the eyes of any passing male. They were a mother and her eighteen-year-old daughter. When asked, the mother, named Mary Dyer, said she was in Terre Haute on business, refusing to elaborate. The pair separated, and Mary went about her mysterious business. The daughter, meanwhile, ended up at Madam Hammond's bagnio and refused to leave when her mother came for her. Mary went to the police to demand they fetch her daughter. She did not have an explanation for why her daughter chose to stay in a brothel. However, her daughter did. She told police her mother ran a bagnio in Crawfordsville, and she also worked there. They had come to Terre Haute to recruit women from Terre Haute bagnios to come work for her. The two were given a hotel room for the night and were escorted to the railway station the next morning.

The Death of Coal Oil Johnny

Sadie Thomas grew up in her mother's brothel and followed in her mother's profession. She grew up not in Terre Haute but in Cincinnati. However, the most pivotal moment of her life took place in a Terre Haute bagnio.

Sadie was born into what some called a hard crowd. Her mother was a longtime madam in the Cincinnati area. Her stepfather was a counterfeiter and rough man who had lounged behind his share of prison walls. Her mother served jail time for passing counterfeit money. Sadie became pregnant at age fifteen courtesy of a young man from a prominent family. He abandoned her. Her older sister Jennie went on to own her own brothel in New York City.

Sadie was an unusually beautiful girl with luxurious brown hair and porcelain skin, and she was always elegantly dressed. It was noted, however, that this young beauty had a fiercely wicked temper, and it was best not to cross her.

In 1879, a handsome, clever man strolled into her mother's brothel. He said his name was Johnny Hall. It was passion at first sight when they met. Before long, they stood before Squire Gilligan, a justice of the peace in Cincinnati, and were married. It is not certain whether she knew then just how famous—or infamous—her new husband was, for she had married the legendary "Coal Oil Johnny."

John Hall, aka John Williams, was the right (or perhaps wrong) man at the right time when the coal oil boom hit Pennsylvania. He delighted in telling his story. He was working as an oxcart driver when the petroleum industry was booming. Somehow, by hook or crook (probably more crook), he suddenly held leases for oil rights that were paying him $3,000 per day.

But Johnny was a big, big spender, never letting money nestle too long in his purse. He said he had squandered almost $1 million. He was dead broke. He, being a clever lad, figured he could always outwit his fellows. He then began a career as one of the best con men in the country. He was not the glib Henry Hill–selling–nonexistent–musical–instruments type of bunko man. Instead, he was a rather quiet fellow who was blessed with a mind made for scheming.

He was an expert gambler who knew how to run a very clever and crooked faro game. He set up phony lotteries, fleeced the suckers and scooted out of town on the next train. People in the nineteenth century were used to all sorts of lotteries, so it was easy to dupe them into thinking Coal Oil Johnny's was legitimate. To be a successful con man, one had to keep moving, and

> **The Days and Doings of "Coal Oil Johnny."**
>
> *From the Terre Haute Saturday Evening Mail.*
>
> Many of our exchanges are full of editorial comments upon a subject which vividly recalls to mind the exciting day of 1858, when poor farmers and land owners of what are now known as the Pennsylvania oil regions, who previously could realize but a few dollars per acre for their land, suddenly found themselves millionaires. It was due to the great oil

The story of Coal Oil Johnny. *Author's collection.*

Johnny had fleeced the gullible from New York to the Mississippi. He was running a crooked faro game in Cincinnati when he met Sadie.

If she initially didn't know what her husband did for a living, she soon found out and joined him in his felonious endeavors. She and her ten-year-old son followed him around the Midwest. To Johnny's credit, he loved his stepson and treated the boy as his own. The trio made their first appearance in Terre Haute in 1882. Johnny was intent on setting up his own gambling den in a city that had so many others. Somehow, it failed; whether this was due to competition or insufficient bankroll is unknown, but Johnny and his family moved on.

They returned to Terre Haute in July 1893. Johnny had a new scheme up his tattered sleeve to try out on the locals. He put up at the St. Charles Hotel with his family and went to meet with an old accomplice who was supposed to bankroll him. He didn't have the money needed for a gambling license and was hoping his friend would help.

Johnny and Sadie's marriage had always been mercurial, to say the least. Both were hot-tempered and quick to take offense. They had raging quarrels at times. Johnny had reputedly tried to kill Sadie twice during their high-pitched fights. Once, when they were back in Cincinnati, Sadie discovered Johnny had gone for comfort in a bagnio. To get his attention and make her husband come home, Sadie went to the brothel and air-conditioned it by putting six bullets through its plate-glass window. Johnny, Sadie, brothels and revolvers were a potent mix.

On the fateful day in Terre Haute, Johnny and Sadie had one of their rows in front of the hotel. She then demanded a satchel he had with him in a hack (a horse-drawn taxi). At first, he was reluctant to give it to her, but he finally relented after taking a revolver out of the bag before handing it over. A witness to the fight said Johnny put his face in his hands and started crying.

To build up his bankroll, Johnny set up a con he was sure would trick the locals—the toothpaste con. Johnny built a circular device that looked something like a roulette wheel. Anyone who bought a packet of toothpaste for a dollar was given a chance to spin and win a prize ranging from one dollar to twenty dollars. Johnny would then set the bait by offering to buy back the chances from his dupes by offering them up to five dollars.

Lest anyone have doubts about the fairness of the game, Johnny had shills in the crowd. They would sell him their chances, and—surprise!—it turned out that they would have won $20. Of course, Johnny had triggered the device under the table with his knee to ensure the wheel stopped at the right place. That day, Johnny made over $300 for his bankroll.

Flush with his success, Johnny decided to hit the town with an accomplice. After drinks at the National Hotel, he and his buddy went drinking and gambling. Johnny lost $110 in a faro game. Feeling that a visit to a brothel or two would be a solace after the gambling losses, the duo set out to make a night of it. After visiting one bagnio, Johnny found himself at Agnes Spencer's place around 12:30 a.m. He ordered another drink and chose Maude Hunter to be his companion for the night and went upstairs with her. After a hedonistic night of drinking and sex, Johnny passed out in the prostitute's bed. He would not awaken again.

Meanwhile, Sadie sat in her hotel room with her son, waiting and waiting and waiting.

Since she had been up most of the previous night making toothpaste packets, she had taken a nap with her son in the afternoon. When she woke up, she looked out the hotel window and saw that Johnny had ended the con for the day, as he was no longer in his spot. She and her son had dinner—no Johnny. She put her son to bed and still no Johnny. Midnight and no Johnny. One o'clock and no Johnny. Anger seeped through her whole body.

At 2:00 a.m., she could no longer stand it. She locked her son in the room and went out. She hired a hack driver to take her on a tour of saloons looking for Johnny. She was in and out of most of the downtown saloons, lingering long enough in a few of them to have a drink. Johnny was not to be found. The driver suggested he go back to his headquarters and see if any of the other drivers had seen him. They learned Johnny had been dropped off at the Spencer bagnio.

Sadie knocked on the bagnio door at 4:00 a.m. At first, she was refused entry by the housekeeper, but Sadie told her to summon the madam. Sadie convinced her that she only wanted to take her husband back to the hotel and was not there to cause trouble. She and the hack driver went upstairs. They found Johnny laying on his left side, his arm across the young prostitute.

Sadie stood in the gloom of the room, silent as a grave. She saw the revolver Johnny had taken out of the satchel was now sitting on the bureau. She calmly picked up the gun and turned to look again upon the tableau of her drunken husband sleeping alongside a young whore. She moved a step closer and pulled the trigger. The bullet entered his chest, glanced off a tendon and then pierced his heart like an arrow. The impact of the bullet pushed him off the bed.

Coal Oil Johnny was literally dead before he hit the floor.

Sadie turned to the driver and asked him to take her back to the hotel. She woke up her son and went down to the lobby. She told the desk clerk to lock up her room. She would not be coming back. Putting her son in the hack, she asked the driver to take her to the jail.

Three days later, she was acquitted of the murder by reason of "emotional insanity." She followed Johnny's body back to Cincinnati for his funeral. The man who bragged he had made and lost almost $1,000,000 had only $7.35 left in his pocket. His friends chipped in to pay for his burial.

The con man left behind one final con job. There was another Coal Oil Johnny who was a legendary oilman, but the Johnny Hall who died in a Terre Haute brothel was not him.

Girls Will Be Girls

Just as prostitutes came in a wide variety of sizes, many also had very different and often vivid personalities. One was Belle (many women adopted Belle as their "professional" name) Story, a woman of unusual physical proportions. Belle was dubbed the "Sandow" of Terre Haute prostitutes. Eugen Sandow was the Arnold Schwarzenegger of the nineteenth century. A German, he was known as the founder of modern bodybuilding and traveled the world showing off his physique and performing feats of strength.

So, you now have an idea of what Belle looked like. She was regarded as the "toughest woman of her class." Belle was often looking for a fight and seldom forewent the opportunity to clench her fists. She would fight all—man, boy or woman—especially after ingesting a few whiskeys in her Amazonian frame. She seemed to relish using her fistic skills on policemen. Terre Haute police knew that arresting Belle was a daunting task.

Officer McGrew learned this in 1896. Sent to quell a disturbance at Mat Wysong's saloon, he encountered Belle in full fury. When he attempted to subdue her, she laid him out with a swift punch to the face. Other officers had to be called to the aid of their prone colleague, whom they found with severely blackened eyes and no doubt a considerable loss of manly pride.

Belle decided she needed to defend her title as Terre Haute's toughest female the next year, but word had spread among the boys in blue in Terre Haute. When Officer Gardner, a tall, well-built policeman, approached the drunken Belle, he was ready for her. She launched a right at Gardner's face, but he parried her thrust with his left arm. Then he knocked her into the street. They tried to put her in the waiting paddy wagon, but Belle had no intention of going quietly. Screaming obscenities, she kicked, scratched and threw more than a few punches. It took all the combined strength of the policemen to finally shove her into the back of the wagon.

But Belle was not done. They still had to transfer her from the wagon to a cell. Belle was a sight when they made it to the jail. She was covered in mud and barely dressed. During the skirmish, her clothes had been ripped and all but torn off. She was basically down to her "nether garments" when police unlatched the door of the paddy wagon. The struggle began anew when the jailer edged her toward her cell. He finally pushed her through the cell door but was rewarded with a kick in the face that left him bloodied.

The next morning, Belle was taken to court, fined for her fisticuffs and returned once more to the West End.

Belle had her match in Nola McClelland, who also worked the West End. Her temper equaled that of Belle's, particularly when her well-known attachment to whiskey filled her veins and eyes with fire. When Nola was drinking, the word went out: stay away. A black prostitute named Gasco did not heed the warning. One night, she made the mistake of riling Nola. She ended up on the sawdust floor after Nola gouged out one of her eyes with a rusty nail. Nola claimed self-defense and was released from custody.

The following year, another member of the bagnio sisterhood, Ella Brown, came up against Nola. It was a year to the day that Brown had shot a client at her bagnio. Whether she was celebrating that event is unknown.

Brown sat drinking and "started out to do the levee." She ended up at the Dell Shafer bagnio, where she spied Nola. Brown immediately started shouting vile names at Nola, who returned her abuse in equally obscene measure. Then, the fight began. As they were rolling around on the floor, Nola pulled a knife from her dress. Three quick thrusts pierced Brown's neck and both shoulders. Once again, Nola prevailed, but this time she feared she had committed murder. She left the house and tried to escape as a doctor tended to Brown's wounds, which were not fatal. Police grabbed Nola as she waited on a train to take her out of town. In the end, Brown made it known that she would not testify against her friend Nola, and the case was dismissed.

The First Madam Brown

Because of her style and ornate, upscale brothel, Edith Brown was the most famous madam in Terre Haute history—but she was not the first Madam Brown. The first was Lulu Brown, and she was probably the most reviled madam in Terre Haute, no doubt because she was black and the white press loathed her.

Lulu Brown was a bit of a larger-than-life character. You knew when she was around as she stalked the streets of the West End. One of her first encounters with the police was in 1885, when she was arrested for robbery; it most certainly was not her last encounter with the authorities.

Madam Brown's bagnio sat along the Wabash River about two blocks south of the county courthouse. It looked like a small three-room house from the outside but was a rambling place once you entered it. It had twelve rooms and was full of doors and "dodgeways" meant to impede the police when they raided the house, as they did in March 1897. The raid resulted from noise complaints about the loud music and the girls parading around in carriages to drum up business. It was documented by the Terre Haute *Semi Weekly Express*, and the reporter's absolute disgust about the "colored" bagnio and its madam was glaringly evident.

Under the headline "Raided a Vile Dive," it lamented the fact that after bail, the women would once again start "befouling the Free Atmosphere." That was the nicest thing said about Lulu and her girls who haunted the "Den of immoral reptiles."

The police arrested "Lulu Brown, a negro wench of infamous reputation," along with four of her "leprous family" of whores with "character many shades darker than their black skin." The bagnio was in a frenzy once the police rushed in. The "inmates" and their "fellow-lepers of the masculine gender" scattered for an exit. More than fifteen hid away or jumped out windows into the cold March night. Police caught three black men as they stumbled out the window, beating them for the effrontery of trying to escape.

Brown, the article said, was a promoter of the "most revolting immorality in the city." She and her pestilential dive were "irredeemably bad." Still, it was never closed down. The reporter opined that police department's hands were tied because someone higher up protected Brown, and worse, this colored viper went free while white madams and prostitutes were routinely arrested.

Peter Bud McCoy came to Terre Haute in the 1880s. He was a penniless horse trader from Marshall County, Indiana. He married Ida Pearman in 1887 but was widowed in 1890. After years of struggle, McCoy saved $130 and bought furniture for the house he shared with his second wife (as there is no record of it, the marriage was likely without benefit of clergy), Flo Thompson. They set up a small bagnio with Flo as the madam.

The brothel was a success, and Bud added a saloon. By 1896, Bud owned at least five other houses in the West End that he rented out as bagnios at a high price. With the West End rapidly filling up, space was at a premium, and McCoy took advantage of it. He often paid the bail and fine when "his girls" were arrested in the occasional sweeps police made through the area to pretend they were trying to control vice in Terre Haute.

Things were seemingly going well for Bud until the fall of 1896. Flo's wandering eye landed on another man. Flo left Bud but retained her desire for her share of the businesses. She sued Bud McCoy, claiming she deserved half of the $25,000 profit they had made. Some thought she and her lawyer were overestimating the income (it was the equivalent of over $600,000 in 2018 dollars). Flo eventually received the bagnio on Second Street and jewelry.

Obviously, the settlement rankled Flo. In January 1897, she went on a rampage. She and a friend, also named Flo, got roaring drunk. Arming themselves with six empty beer bottles, they set out in search of their prey. Their target was the front window of Bud's saloon. Their early drinking bout did not hamper their aim. Six bottles smashed through the window, with one of them almost parting Bud's hair.

Their shouts filled the street until Bud rushed to confront them. He knocked both Flos to the street. He turned his attention to his ex-wife and landed blows to her mouth, both eyes and her nose. He scratched her for good measure. No one came to their aid. Bud finally let them up, and both made their escape (with Flo Thompson sporting blood on her face). Flo and Flo continued their evening, bouncing from saloon to saloon. It was not long before they were helplessly drunk and stumbling through the streets. A policeman sent for the paddy wagon, and they were taken to jail to sleep it off.

You would think that his bad luck with women would have tempered Bud McCoy's feelings for the fairer sex. But he took up with a woman named Ella, again without benefit of clergy. It did not take long for that relationship to flounder. In October 1897, Ella disappeared. Dressing as a man, she stuffed $800 in her trouser pocket and called for a hack, which dropped her off at a house. When questioned, the hack driver refused to reveal Ella's location.

Bud McCoy was finished with his grasping clotheshorse new wife. He began throwing her belongings out onto the street. Enough shoes to fill a barrel were joined by enough dresses and bonnets to stock a store on Second Street. They were soon gathered up by eager men and women. The police later captured Ella at the Big Four railroad depot. Bud took back what was left of the $800, and Ella went her own way.

The Gathering

A German immigrant named Volger operated a bagnio in Terre Haute. She was not well liked. Most considered her pushy and extremely vulgar. In 1883, she opened a new brothel on the south end of town very near a new residential neighborhood. Her new bagnio was called the Farm. It was located in the country south of present-day Fifth and Hulman Streets. The residential area featured large Victorian houses. It would eventually be known as Farrington Grove and housed some of the better sort of Terre Haute.

Volger was despised by the police because she played cat-and-mouse games with them. After an unsuccessful raid, the police took her on again the next night. Two paddy wagons carried a group of policemen back down to the bagnio. Volger saw and heard them coming and locked the house tight. She forgot that one of her girls, Rose Elmore, was still out gathering wood from the shed. Two officers planted themselves at the rear of the house after arresting Rose. Several other officers banged on the door, declaring that they had a warrant.

Volger called their bluff by saying that if they really did have a warrant, they would have to knock down the door, as she wasn't going to let them in. If they could not show her the warrant, they could just head back to town. Frustrated, the police went back to headquarters.

This time, they came back with not only a warrant but with police chief Fasig, who busted down two doors to force his way into the house. Volger looked at them slyly and said it was all for nothing. There was no one in the house except her mother and daughter. Fasig sent two policemen upstairs to look around, where they encountered more locked doors. They heard a noise behind a door and shouted to open it or they would kick it in. Those inside yelled they couldn't because they didn't have a key, and if they kicked it, the door would smash them.

When they called down for a key, Volger again said she did not have one. She finally relented and said her little girl Gussie had it. Back upstairs went the police. When the door opened, they found two girls in what looked like a hidden closet. Soon, they were all sitting in the paddy wagon on their way to jail.

After a series of continuances, Volger agreed to leave town as soon as she could rent or sell her house. Someone was prevailed to rent the house for five years, and Volger went to St. Louis. She told people she was going to open a beauty parlor. A year later, she was operating a brothel in St. Louis.

The *Saturday Evening Mail* took note of the Volger move. It published an editorial saying that prostitution was a "fact that the social evil cannot be eradicated, and must be confined in as small a limit as possible." It was one of the first pragmatic steps to creating a red-light district. Others in Terre Haute and the nation were advocating much the same thing.

The idea was simple. If you limit vice to a prescribed area, it would benefit the community. If there was a specific area set aside for purveyors of vice, then it could not just be stumbled upon, and those who wished to go there knew what they were getting. If they chose to go to a red-light district, it was up to them to keep out of trouble. Additionally, confining vice to a small area theoretically made it easy for police and governmental agencies to control it.

This was the first halting step toward the creation of the West End. By 1900, the district was forming. At its zenith, it was an area of thirty or more blocks bordered on the west by the Wabash River. It was there that many brothels, saloons and gambling dens had clustered for years. It was the ideal area to house as much vice as the city could contain within its boundaries.

The West End would become a little community of its own and the area that would make Terre Haute infamous nationwide as a "sin city."

CURSE OF THE WHITE QUEEN OF CHINATOWN

Terre Haute had an opium problem. It was, said a local paper in 1887, caught in "vile dens of oriental vice." The article explained that opium was a "discovery of the chinks," Chinese immigrants who brought dope habits to the country. By 1910, it had gotten worse.

So how did a small Midwestern town become home to so many addicts and a center for the opium trade? Part of the answer might lay with the "White Queen of Chinatown."

Rose Sybell was born in 1868 in Cleveland, Ohio, but moved to Lafayette, Indiana, with her family as a child. There, her family doctor, who also became her lover, introduced her to opium as a teenager. They eventually set up an opium den near the Lahr House Hotel in downtown Lafayette. Rose lured young women from the area into the den, where dozens became addicted. At any one time, she said, you could find seven or eight young women lolling in the den, often naked.

After the death of her doctor/lover, Sybell operated the den for another year before the police decided to banish her from town. She said she was not prosecuted because many of the young women in the den were from prominent families who did not want a public scandal if the case went to court.

Sybell then took her supplies of opium 100 miles down the Wabash River to Terre Haute, where she set up a new den. She supposedly did so with the cooperation of a Chinese tong, a secret criminal society responsible for

> **WHITE QUEEN OF CHINATOWN.**
>
> Tells Horrible Story of Life With the Chinese in an Opium Den.
>
> American Girl Leads Life of Shame and Dishonor With the Yellow Devils.

Article detailing the life of Rose Sybell. *Author's collection.*

much of the opium trafficking in the United States. Her new den was near the infamous "colored" brothel run by Lulu Brown. Business was good, and she was soon drawing customers from as far away as 100 miles.

She hired two Chinese workers to "cook" the opium. The cooks introduced her to Yo Wang Quan. Yo was supposedly an Eastern-educated ringleader of the tong who spoke fluent English. He quickly became smitten with Sybell and plied her with expensive gifts. He convinced her to go to New York and marry him. She agreed but also insisted on two ceremonies. One was a Taoist marriage ceremony and the other a civil ceremony, because she wanted to be married the American way, too.

Shortly afterward, they returned to Terre Haute, but Yo convinced her she needed brighter lights than Terre Haute could offer. She sold her "business" and moved to Chicago.

Yo's tong put up the money to open a new den to be managed by Sybell. It was, she felt, "the finest joint ever operated in the United States." Yo smuggled two Chinese women into the United States to process the opium, and Sybell had them train men to do the job. The new den "soon became one of the sights in Chicago." All was going well—the proper Chicago police palms had been greased, and business swelled. But a crusading newspaper editor named Dunlap put so much heat on the operation that it was forced to shut down.

Sybell then moved to Philadelphia. She had no way of knowing that her move to the City of Brotherly Love would ultimately lead to her downfall.

The Six Companies, a tong, had her manage a den at 934 Race Street. It became a great favorite among the more prosperous merchants in Chinatown, who treated her with great respect. Three years into her tenure at the den, she received word that Yo was dead and his body had been sent back to China. Taoist priests showed her what they said was Yo's will. She was not entitled to an inheritance, they said, and they stripped her house bare, taking all her jewelry and furniture.

Sybell then turned to the merchants who had frequented her place. They obliged and set her up in business again. She then married Lee Tong Yuen. Her second marriage was short-lived. Lee returned to China, and by Chinese custom, Sybell was free again. She became known as "the White Queen of Chinatown," and visitors flocked to the den.

On May 16, 1901, Rose received a visit from four Chinese men wanting to smoke. She told them she did not allow "Chinks" to "hit" in her house and told them to go to the Walla Walla den that catered to Chinese addicts. They did not seem offended. Instead, they stayed to play cards and then left.

They later returned with three Taoist priests who bore word that Lee had died in China and they had come to get what was his. Sybell stood her ground. She was not about to have everything taken from her again. Eventually, all agreed to let Lee Toy, "mayor of Chinatown," decide the "case." They all then sat down to smoke opium. One of the priests sent out for food. After eating, Rose blacked out, later waking to find herself being beaten with a curtain rod by one of the priests. She passed out again, and when she came to, she was nearly naked and sprawled in an alley. She was found and taken to the police station and then a hospital. There, she made her deathbed statement, and she died the next day.

One senses the fine hand of a newspaper reporter in this story. Sybell's deathbed statement was very coherent and precise considering her condition. Every fact and place mentioned in the article are verifiable. But in some ways, it seems too perfect, as if the reporter might have been stretching things a bit to make his point. Still, Sybell's story was very representative of the opium trade at the time

Opium, cocaine and morphine were well known in Terre Haute long before the arrival of the White Queen. All were basically legal. The first federal laws regarding these drugs were not passed until 1915, and they were primarily

Lee Toy, "Mayor of Chinatown." *Author's collection.*

enacted to tax the drugs. Opium, in particular, had long been an ingredient in patent medicines and was said to cure a vast assortment of ailments. Laudanum, a derivative of opium, was often used to calm cranky or teething children. Opium-laced medicines were prescribed for all sorts of "female complaints," including hysteria. This was why there were a higher number of women opium smokers than might be expected of the "fairer sex" during the period.

As early as 1887, there were reports of opium-laced cigarettes appearing in Terre Haute. In those times, the opium came as much from doctors as from opium smugglers. Doctors could make a lot of money by prescribing vast amounts of the drug. The Sears catalog offered to mail you cocaine and a syringe for $1.50. Addicts didn't have to leave their homes to grab their high.

Opium gave users a sense of euphoria for hours. It was a pipeline to "dreamland." After a time, the drug wore off, and the user settled into what seemed like a trance, thus the images of smokers appearing to be asleep or doped for hours afterward. It promoted a serene sense of languor. A Terre Haute newspaper offered readers a primer on opium smoking in 1897:

> *The "layout" for smoking opium consists first of a large stem, made of bamboo. This stem is between 2½ to 3 inches in circumference. Almost midway of the stem sets a large clay bowl with only a small hole, such as would be made by a large darning needle. Then there is a small lamp, which burns peanut or olive oil; then the yen hok, about the shape of a darning needle, to cook the opium with and other like instruments for cleaning the pipe, and last the opium itself in a small jar or tol.*

The article ended by saying most of the equipment came from a large importing house in Philadelphia and could be purchased in at least one Chinese store in Terre Haute.

Opium was a growth industry in Terre Haute. In 1904, a Chinese man came to town with the idea of opening another den. He wanted a prime location on the main street, Wabash Avenue. The den would be hidden by a "blind" of other goods. That ruse was used by cigar stores in town, which hid their gambling operations from the public using stocks of cigars and windows filled with girlie cards and posters. When told such a storefront would cost between $1,300 and $3,000 per year to rent, the Chinese man did not blink an eye. Opium was indeed a growth business.

Opium-smoking first made inroads in the West End, where it joined booze, cocaine and women's bodies as articles of commerce. Brothels, saloons and gambling dens joined the dirty streets as places to buy a ticket to dreamland. Its early adoptees were prostitutes, drunks and others looking for escape, even if for just a while.

But its use was assuredly not limited to the "low characters" of Terre Haute. The poor addicts "on the hog," as it was known, had to steal to support their habits. It began to be a drug of choice for more and more of the wealthier sort. One dealer told a reporter that people would be amazed at the number of high-class users in town. One wealthy couple had gone so far as to install their own private opium den in their home, where they smoked every night. The dealer had to make regular trips to their house to keep them supplied with the drug.

At least one—perhaps more—of the "ladies who lunch" crowd also took up the pipe. These were the wives of prominent well-to-do men in town who sought more from life than a *Good Housekeeping* seal of approval. Some would make daily visits to the upscale dens in Terre Haute. No slumming in the West End for these ladies. They would drop by for an hour of smoking and then gather themselves up enough to go home and make sure dinner was on the table when their husbands got home.

Such drug stories often carried the inevitable cautionary tale of a "good girl gone bad." In this case, it was a girl from a good family in a town near Terre Haute. She took to traveling to the big city of Terre Haute in search of some excitement. A sense of romance and adventure drove her to cautiously walk into an opium den for the first time. She enjoyed the novelty and experiences there. Soon, she was coming back for more and more of the drug. The opium octopus soon caught her in its many-tentacled grasp. The pretty girl became pale-faced and "dopey" looking. Her secret was discovered, and she was shunned by family and friends. She drifted into the West End, where her earnings as a prostitute went toward purchasing opium.

Terre Haute was not only a city of users, it was a supplier. While local authorities may have turned a blind eye, the feds did not. A 1911 federal raid on an opium factory in a Chinese laundry run by James Moy found it could produce seven gallons of "gum" in a matter of days, enough to supply dens within a five-hundred-mile radius. The Internal Revenue Service commissioner declared that Terre Haute was a center for opium manufacture and smuggling, along with New York, Chicago, San Francisco and Seattle. The Terre Haute police chief said the feds were overstating the problem, and Terre Haute had it under control.

If so, it soon spun out of control again. Two more federal raids in 1916 again found a full-scale manufacturing operation. The feds also found a doctor who was issuing so many prescriptions that he was flooding the market. He kindly added an instruction sheet to tell users how to make it into pills for easy use.

The raid led to talk of prosecutions. This sent Terre Haute politicians scurrying to Indianapolis to stop indictments. The reason they gave was that prosecutions would further taint the city's reputation. It was more likely they were trying to protect some of their campaign donors. No prosecutions ensued.

The federal raids did not eliminate the use or manufacturing of opium, it just drove it further into the shadows. Opium use would continue (and would be joined by other drugs) over the years.

THE OTHER WEST END

There were numerous reasons the West End became the red-light district in Terre Haute. First, it was already the site of saloons, gambling dens and numerous brothels. Second, the people who lived there were powerless to do anything about it. No one cared if they did not wish to be the vice district. They were the poorest of the poor who lived in a disease-infested slum. Their west end was bisected by what one charity group called a "highway of poverty, shame and filth."

The area along the riverfront on either side of the Wabash River Bridge was always a rough place. At one point, the Terre Haute Crematorium was located on the west bank of the river. Slaughterhouses were scattered along both riverbanks. It was filled with warehouses serving river traffic and railroads, shanties for the poor and the city dump.

It was a stench-filled, ugly plot of land teeming with gamblers, whores, petty criminals and thieves. Highwaymen haunted the area, preying on travelers passing through and the men who went to the bagnios. The robbers logically assumed that those two groups in particular had money in their pockets.

Assaults, brawls and thievery were nightly occurrences. Murders were frequent. Random, ugly violence could erupt at any time. This was the case in 1905, when a young boy was murdered in a gambling room above a saloon. The cause of the argument was unclear, but an older man beat the boy to death with a cuspidor. It was reported that the games only stopped for long enough to remove the body.

In short, the West End was a slum filled with poorly built, unsanitary tenements. Families of up to ten lived in one or two shabby rooms. Many of these ramshackle buildings were within 100 yards of the county courthouse. Indoor plumbing was but a dream for the residents. Outhouses were breeding places for sky-darkening swarms of insects. Some residents simply emptied their slop buckets out the window, where human waste mixed with the mud on the streets. Children played in this squalid mist. Within an area filled with saloons, brothels and cadres of thieves, rapists and killers, the virtue of young girls was unprotected. And who owned this quagmire? Some of the better sort of Terre Haute, including bankers, wealthy businessmen and striving politicians, among them the venal, corrupt Donn Roberts, future disgraced mayor.

Believe it or not, there was an even worse area on the opposite bank of the Wabash River.

People of the Dump

There was no place more reviled in Vigo County than Taylorville. Taylorville was quite literally built on a dump, and most viewed those who lived there as little more than human debris. It and its people were seen as the flotsam that washed up along the west bank of the Wabash across from Terre Haute. According to many, Taylorville was home to ragpickers, thieves, whores and the diseased. It was 60 acres of hell.

Taylorville is located south of the National Road along the bottomlands between Terre Haute and West Terre Haute. It was supposedly named after "Captain" Taylor, a farmer who lived on Ferguson Hill near West Terre Haute. Taylor's connection to the hamlet that bears his name, or how he became a "captain," is unknown.

The first settlers were squatters, people looking for some kind of home. The place left to them was near the Terre Haute dump. They built their crude houses from whatever scraps of wood, tin or brick washed up on the riverbank. They scrounged the dump for food to feed their children and scraps of metal, rags or other items they could sell to eke out a sort of living.

Taylorville's plight was highlighted by the Indiana State Board of Health in March 1913, shortly after the Great Flood of 1913. It called the place "the Peril of Terre Haute." This article described the "hovels" in which people lived and how they were often driven from those ramshackle homes several times a year by flooding. The people, it said, "were of the American gypsy type" who subsisted as "ragpicker, push-cart, slop-wagon driver" types.

To eat, they gathered anew after each new dumping of discards from restaurants and stores. "It is a familiar sight when the dump has received a new supply of garbage to see men, women and children…delving arm deep in such material for food for their tables. Half-rotten oranges, and other fruits, pieces of bread soaked in the slops from some hotel, decaying scraps of meat—all are seized with avidity and carried away to the filthy places, their homes, where they eat, live and have their living."

In short, they lived amid filth and squalor. People and animals often lived under the same shaky roofs, sharing the spaces with "countless billions of flies." Sanitation was all but unknown. Their water came from the river or fetid wells. Disease was their constant companion. The report particularly noted widespread gonorrhea and syphilis, even among the young, in these "derelicts of humankind."

There is no doubt that Taylorville was a crowded, unruly place that at best disdained the law. It was crowded with rough saloons, gambling and drug dens and hideouts for an ever-changing troupe of felons. Across the river from one of the most booming red-light districts in the Midwest (the West End), it had more than its share of prostitutes and brothels, which were often just dilapidated one-room shacks. If the fleeting affections and bodies of women could be bought on the cheap in Terre Haute, there was always someone in Taylorville who would beat the price.

Perhaps the absolute worst place was just across the river bridge near the Terre Haute city dump. Amid hovels that were little more than lean-tos was a grimy, crime-ridden little tent city. Some of the tents were little more than portable bagnios. One was the domain of an unwashed, haggard "river bottom prostitute" simply known as Mrs. Cooper. Police searching for Mrs. Cooper's murderous "husband" came upon her tent. It was guarded by a pack of starving, savage dogs. Inside the tent was a group of women strewn upon the dirt floor. They were sickly-looking women wearing barely enough clothing "to protect their modesty, if they possessed such article" of humanity. These places were lowliest of the low, where a woman's body could be bought for as little as a dime or a half-eaten loaf of bread. It was degradation at its worst.

The West End's version of Taylorville was Jockey Alley.

Jockey Alley was so named because it was once the center for horse traders. The alley's "homes" were dilapidated sheds, lean-tos and houses that seemed poised to lose their battle with gravity at any moment. The

"All we saw in the store were two women clerks and a young man with sore eyes."

Taylorville shanty. *Indiana State University Archives.*

area's houses might have one window and barely-hinged doors. They were leaky, wind-whipped hovels with rotting floors that housed malnourished, disease-wracked people. It was the definition of poverty.

Jane Porter was seventy years old. She had lived in Jockey Alley for fifteen years, and some called her the "Queen of Jockey Alley." She lived in a shack that cost her twenty dollars per year, and she was known as one of the best foragers in the alley. She always seemed to find tossed-away food, shoes or scraps of clothing. Like many, she spent part of her days begging. She was also known for having the cleanest house in the alley.

A few doors down from Jane Porter was a family that exemplified life in the alley. They lived in a shack with a crudely cut half-sash window that allowed the only light into the house. It was covered with newspaper, not glass. The air in the shed seemed congealed from a mix of clothes washed in lye and rancid grease and human waste. The family's food supply consisted of what could be scavenged from scraps thrown out by restaurants, grocery stores and commission houses.

The husband had been sick and unable to work or care for himself. A boarder lived with the family. He, too, was unable to care for himself and lived with them in exchange for his meager Civil War pension. When asked where he slept, he showed that life had not robbed him of a sense of humor:

"Oh, they hang me on a hook at night." The only decoration in the house was a toy violin that was scavenged from somewhere. The rent was two dollars per month.

Despite the hell that was their daily lives, there was a sense of community in Jockey Alley. Everyone was saddened when Jane Porter was taken to the pest house after contracting smallpox during a 1903 epidemic. She would never return to the alley.

By 1907, charity groups were intent on forcing owners to raze the buildings and trying to find new homes for the residents. This opened up more places to build brothels. The West End, the red-light district of sin city, was now firmly in place.

DUH MAYOR

Donn Roberts strutted through life, toupee precariously perched atop his head. Born in Annapolis, Illinois, in 1869, his family moved to Terre Haute when he was young. "He always had his way in everything," a friend later noted. There were "no curbs" put on him. This was an interesting phrase, as Roberts later installed a lot of curbs as a contractor. He graduated from Rose Polytechnic Institute in 1889 as a civil engineer.

Roberts was a man on the make. Within a few years, he was a prominent contractor and was making a lot of money. Knowing the way things worked in Terre Haute, he became heavily involved in local politics—not an arena one entered unless he was prepared to get his hands dirty. He eventually became the chairman of the Terre Haute Democratic Party. He used his political influence and more than a few under-the-table bribes to gain valuable city and county construction contracts.

His company paved the grade between Terre Haute and West Terre Haute and sewer extensions for the city. He successfully "bid" on projects to pave city streets. Roberts acquired property all over Terre Haute, especially in the West End. He was a slumlord who gouged rent from those unfortunate enough to have to live in his squalid houses along the river. Even though he was a contractor, much-needed repairs to the tenements never seemed to get done. He owned lots that contained saloons and brothels.

Despite shoddy work that often had to be redone, Roberts continued to receive city contracts. He was even named city engineer (though he was later fired from the job). He became a wealthy and powerful man. A natural schemer, he soon hooked up with underworld figures like Buster Clark, using them to help him "fix" elections.

Roberts was easily elected mayor in 1913. Some felt his victory was due more to his stance against the despised Terre Haute Traction Company than his agenda. Donn Roberts serving as mayor did not sit well with some. Political opponents, well aware that Roberts paid for "floaters" to vote early and often, pressed to have him indicted for election fraud. A Terre Haute jury found him not guilty of voter fraud during the 1913 elections. But there were others with political influence, and a federal court indicted Roberts and scores of others for election tampering in 1915. It was a strange trial that included "Bat" Masterson, dynamite and a pretty woman.

David "Bat" Masterson was a prizefighter and private detective turned labor "slugger." Labor sluggers were men hired by company management to intimidate workers or unions. In this case, the company was the Terre Haute Traction Company. Masterson took part in burglarizing the hotel room of a streetcar union organizer in Indianapolis. Masterson and a Terre Haute Traction Company officer were later indicted for that little caper. In a plot that would rival those of the Soviet secret service, Masterson considered hiring a female detective to ensnare Roberts in a "honey trap." The idea was for her to maneuver Roberts into a compromising position so they could blackmail him.

But Masterson changed sides. He was later indicted by a Vigo County grand jury for plotting to dynamite the homes of Special Judges Charles Fortune and Felix Blankenbaker and Special Prosecutor Roach. That plot never materialized. Instead, Masterson fired shots into the window of Blankenbaker's home. He was indicted by a Vigo County grand jury. Upon being arrested, Masterson jokingly said, "I was hired to keep Donn out of jail, and now it looks like I will be convicted." "Bat" was eventually given a fifteen-dollar fine and released.

But Roberts was indeed convicted of election fraud, along with what seemed like half of the Terre Haute Democratic Party. More than eighty officials pleaded guilty and were given fines. Roberts and twenty-one others were found guilty and sentenced to do time at the Leavenworth federal prison. Roberts was given the longest sentence, and as the leader, was among the first fourteen of his coconspirators sent to Kansas by train. But even then, he was cosseted as he and the others were treated with great deference by the guards. There was a sense of near-frivolity on the train. That ended when the prison gate clanged behind them, and all of a sudden, reality set in.

But still, the Terre Haute 22 were treated very well. Warden Thomas Morgan greeted them personally. They were given isolation cells that were four times larger than the tiny cells for "regular" prisoners. Roberts played the showman. When the new inmates received their prison haircuts, he simply pulled off his toupee. It made him "look like a white billiard ball, fringed with fuzz at the base." He was given a prison skullcap to cover his naked pate. When the group entered the lunch hall, Roberts spotted the warden and Terre Haute reporters in the visitor's balcony. He entertained them by doing a quick tango.

Roberts' second day in prison was a big one. First, his toupee was returned to him, and he was given the honor of throwing out the first pitch of the prison baseball season. The honor was at the request of former professional baseball player Danny Clare. Clare was in Leavenworth because he was convicted of white slavery. Some of the other Hautean prisoners quickly looked for their own recreational activities. Elmer Talbott had been a bandmaster in Terre Haute and asked to join the prison band. He was joined by George Sovern, who fancied himself a drummer.

The warden then announced the prison jobs to which the group would be assigned. Most were given easy jobs. Dennis Shea, who had been a blacksmith before becoming chief of the Terre Haute police, was assigned as a farrier in the prison stables. Roberts was assigned to the construction engineer's office—a very nice prison job. But Roberts's haughtiness soon got him in trouble. He was disciplined for his comportment by being demoted to garden work.

But Roberts being Roberts, he just couldn't let well enough alone. "With all the offended dignity at his command," he took himself to the warden's office to complain about the laundry. He said the laundry was not giving proper service to his clothes (he was not required to always wear a uniform like other prisoners). The warden was not amused. He basically said if Roberts could do a better job, he should join the laundry to show them how it was done. He demoted Roberts once again, which meant he also lost privileges like recreation time.

Friends said the banishment almost made Roberts lose his mind. He became despondent and was acting "queerly." The worst part, he wrote home, was that he had to sort dirty clothes alongside "negroes and Chinese" convicts.

Roberts finally saw that he must feign some humility to get himself out of the steamy laundry. That, along with pressure from his politician friends, got him back in good graces with the warden. He was given a cushy job as office messenger in the prison clerk's office. The rest of his term was in the country-club atmosphere accorded to white-collar prisoners. Roberts later claimed he never spent a day locked in a cell and was free to move about the prison.

With his friends back home constantly trying to get his sentence commuted, he was sure he would soon be released. He even fired telegrams back to Terre Haute in which he acted if he was still mayor. In one, he ordered that the police force should be cut back, as it was costing too much money. He also arranged for many of his family and cronies to be given city jobs. He talked of running for mayor again, or even for governor. But he was not to get off easy. As the other Terre Haute prisoners were paroled, he stayed behind. He was the last one paroled. He was released in October 1918 after serving a little over half of his minimum sentence.

He returned home to cheering fans, thinking he would still be a power with which to be reckoned. He offered his service to the federal government, which was still at war, explaining that he had learned foreign languages while in prison. He was certain his supposed fluency in German, French and Spanish could help the war effort. No such job was offered. He was disbarred after his conviction. The new generation of Terre Haute Democrats kept their distance.

Roberts's old machine had fractured while he was imprisoned, and he decidedly lost a bid for reelection to mayor in 1921. He continued to run for the office until 1925, when the U.S. Supreme Court upheld an Indiana law that declared anyone convicted of a felony and who had served time in a federal prison was ineligible to run for elected office, though he continued to try for years afterward.

He was arrested for assault in 1926 when he knocked down a seventeen-year-old messenger boy for brushing up against his clothes. The messenger tried to tell Roberts it was not done on purpose, as he was trying to avoid hitting another pedestrian. Evidently, this excuse was not good enough for Roberts, as he continued to hit and kick the boy while he was prostrate on the ground and unable to defend himself. One wonders what might have befallen the young lad had he dislodged Roberts's toupee in the incident. This came on the heels of another assault charge the previous year. Roberts restarted his construction business and was once again receiving city and country contracts when a man he fired tried to argue it was without cause. The ex-mayor beat the ex-employee with a sledgehammer handle. He paid fines and restitution to the victims to avoid a jail sentence. Roberts was one of those men whose temper did not mellow with age. In 1929, he was again charged with assault after striking a truck driver in an argument over a parking spot.

In 1930, he came up with a new moneymaking plan. He had been operating a filling station at Second and Wabash Streets for years when a dusty light bulb appeared above his head to signify his new brainstorm. He outfitted car bodies to be mobile filling stations. Always thinking he deserved an edge, he would "park" his "stations" on land on which the state had right of way. When they ordered him off the land, he claimed squatter's rights. He was eventually convicted of embezzling state gas tax funds and given a two-to-five-year sentence. After a failed appeal, he was ordered to the state penitentiary. His term there lasted only two weeks. His health quickly deteriorated, and he was sent home for humanitarian reasons.

He was only home for a short time before he suffered a heart attack and died on August 2, 1936.

KING OF THE VICE TRUST

Frank "Buster" Clark was the Renaissance man of the Terre Haute underworld. Pimp, drug dealer, bootlegger, thief, saloon owner, gambler, political fixer, fence, thug, tax cheat—Buster did it all. He had so many fingers in so many illicit pies that he needed a third hand. Local newspapers began writing about a "vice trust" that controlled all aspects of vice in Terre Haute. Clark was the king of that trust.

Born in Illinois in 1874, Buster Clark appeared in Terre Haute in the 1890s. He was a big man—very big for his era. He was a tall, well-built and imposing figure. It must have run in the family, as his sister was described as a very big lady. He came under the tutelage of Bud McCoy, who owned West End saloons and had an interest in several brothels. Clark worked as a bouncer, bartender and muscle for the one-time horse trader and learned the ways of life in the West End. He learned the lessons quite well. It did not take him long to become a figure in the West End. In a place that was filled with tough guys and those on the make, he soon made a name for himself.

He was no stranger to the police. He was arrested twenty-eight times between 1897 and 1912, most often for assault but also for theft and associating with prostitutes.

He was arrested for the first time in 1897 when he was hauled in after a brawl in the notorious Bud McCoy saloon. It seems that some good ol' boys from Paris, Illinois, sauntered into McCoy's place on Labor Day with the intention of drinking it dry. Thirst slaked, minds numbed, liquid courage bubbling through their veins, the five country toughs announced that they

Ed Light's place, a typical West End saloon, circa 1910. *Vigo County Historical Society.*

did not intend to part with their hard-earned money to pay for their drinks. Instead, they would fight Bud and Buster for the tab. This was not well accepted by the offended saloon owner. The fight was on.

Now, the West End was not a stranger to fights. No doubt, several impromptu bouts a day took place in its dives and dirty streets. Such a thing was as predictable as the sun rising and setting. Soon, chairs were pushed back, glasses tumbled and fists flew as McCoy's boys upheld the sanctity of commerce. The walls could not hold the growing brawl.

As bodies began spilling onto the streets, word went out and shouts of "Fight! Fight!" echoed along the streets. Doors flung open, living rooms emptied and excited spectators rushed for ringside perches. They were not disappointed. The original gladiators were soon joined by onlookers. Why miss a chance for a good fight, even if you didn't know which side you were on?

Small battles took place along many fronts. A wiry little guy pounced on Buster's back, arms encircling the big man's neck. Buster was having a hard time shaking him off until one of his associates grabbed a loose board and pile-drove it into the little guy. A reporter noted "blood flowing like water from a street sprinkler." By then, the ruckus had attracted a bevy of billy club–toting police. Had it been available, they would have donned full riot gear. They had been through West End brawls before. Some sort of order was restored, though it took a while.

Missing were the boys from Paris. They had gleefully headed back to Illinois without paying for their drinks. That would teach those Terre Haute city slickers. Bud and Buster were hauled off to jail, but they did not stay there for long.

In January 1903, Buster and his girlfriend Maude Tate sauntered into Eva Robinson's brothel on Second Street intent on trouble. Robinson had done something that deeply offended Tate. You did not do that sort of thing to Buster's girl. Clark wasted no time in tossing the madam to the floor and then turned it over to Maude, exhorting her to cut Robinson's throat. Sharpened hat pins flashed through the air, joining curses and clawing fingernails. Several people tried to halt the melee, but Clark vowed to "knock the head off" anyone who tried to separate the brawling women. Finally, the police intervened.

Clark and Tate were charged with assault. When he appeared before a judge, Clark offered to plead guilty and pay the twenty-five-dollar fine. Such a plea went against Buster's coarse grain, but he said he wanted to avoid a trial, which would damage his reputation! The judge would have none of that. Clark was put on trial and was not only fined the twenty-five dollars but was sentenced to jail.

Two years later, an attorney named Siegel Hughes had the temerity to summon Clark to testify in a court case. That a mere lawyer would summon the King of the West End greatly offended Clark. He reluctantly went to the courthouse. Around 11:00 a.m., the court took a short recess. Hughes was walking to the stairs when Clark grabbed him and knocked down the lawyer. Clark then set about beating him, leaving Hughes in a puddle of his own blood. Clark, his feelings made clear, headed back to his saloon. He had to be dragged back by the police. Clark's little fracas cost him a one-hundred-dollar fine, but he was let go, no doubt figuring it was money well spent.

Buster Clark steadily rose to power in a West End that was undergoing change. He bought a saloon, opened roadhouses and may have had a stake in a brothel or two. Perhaps his most lucrative ventures were gambling and stealing. He gathered a gang around him. Men stole for him, ran gambling operations and collected the protection money he extorted from those who wanted to do business in his kingdom. There were slot machines in his saloons and roulette and cards in the back rooms. Buster was making a lot

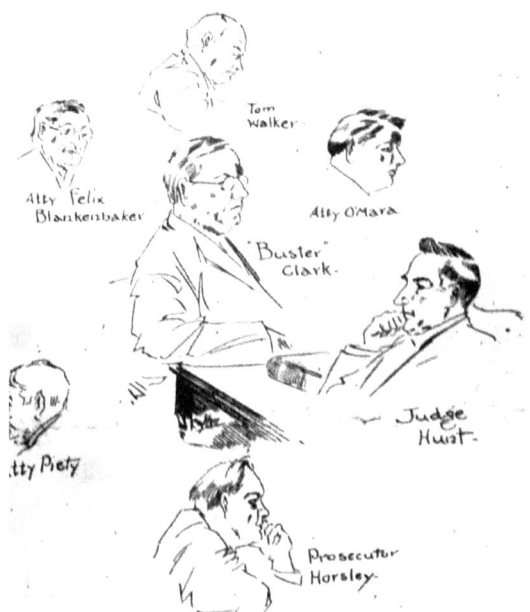

Cartoon about the Buster Clark slot machine trial. *Vigo County Historical Society*.

of money, and his power grew. By 1905, he was known as the "King of the West End."

Terre Haute politics was an especially corrupt arena in the early twentieth century. If an honest election took place during the era, it was purely by mistake. The 1915 elections were worse than most.

Clark's influence over the West End made him a power broker in the shady world of Terre Haute politics. So adept was he that he managed to get a politician who was so deep in his pocket he lived among the lint elected as prosecutor.

A die-hard Republican, Buster was so adept at vote-rigging that he could have taught a graduate seminar in the subject. This was true in the tainted 1915 elections. Mayor Donn Roberts, an especially corrupt and venal contractor with a long history of bribery and fixed bids that he used to attain public works projects, coerced Clark into coordinating vote-buying in the West End precincts by threatening to close down his saloon. That he was forced to help Democrats must have been especially galling to Clark. He simply hated Democrats.

Roberts gave Clark cash to pay six hundred "floaters" to assure the election. Floaters were people who were paid to float between different polling places and vote as many times as they could. Clark enlisted the aid of George Evans, Madam Lulu Brown's husband, to get out the (colored) vote. Evans conducted a class at his saloon to instruct floaters about how to vote several times. Clark went through the area handing out cash or tokens that could be redeemed for drinks at Clark's or Evans's saloon.

Clark gave cash to a black man named Louis Watkins to go voting. After voting at three different places, Watkins repaired to the Evans saloon, where he won forty-two dollars shooting craps. It was his big day. With the cash in his pocket, he felt he no longer had to vote. Instead, he made twelve or fourteen trips from the saloon escorting floaters to the polls.

Clark spent election day overseeing the operation. He had to advise one of his men to be careful about the names he was putting on the fake voter registration cards. It seems he was using the same names multiple times, and Clark was afraid some snoopy poll worker would get wise to the fraud. Yes, Buster Clark knew what he was doing, and Roberts got the results he wanted.

Later that year, Roberts and the others were convicted of election fraud during the 1914 elections. Roberts was sentenced to six years in Leavenworth federal prison.

The Case of the Missing Slot Machines

There were two slot machine "trusts" in Terre Haute. The biggest was run by Buster Clark and his faithful lieutenants Eddie Gosnell and George Sovern. The smaller one was under the control of Tommy Moore and his men. The two groups were on friendly terms and did not poach on each other's territories. There was also a group of independent saloon owners who bought their own slot machines and refused to pay "tribute" to either trust. This situation rankled Clark and Gosnell. It was bad enough that they were not getting a bigger slice of the gambling pie, but they couldn't stand the gall of independents thinking they could thumb their noses at the King of the West End.

In 1917, Clark sent his minions on a burglary spree. His men broke into the offending saloons and stole their slots. Their haul was taken to a back room at Buster's saloon. There, one of his men, Harry Barker, set about changing the numbers on the slots and further disguising them. They were then stored at Clark's cottage in north Terre Haute.

While they were at it, Clark's boys also stole automobiles and repainted them. Nothing was too small for Buster, as he also had them steal tires. He was a man with an eye for profit. But that caper finally got Clark indicted.

Slot machine seized in Terre Haute, circa 1920. *Indiana Historical Society.*

The case dragged on for two years through three trials. In the end, Buster was acquitted.

However, what the state could not do (send Clark to prison), the feds would accomplish a year later.

The drug scene continued to flourish in Terre Haute. Heroin, morphine, cocaine and opium were hot sellers in the West End and elsewhere. Then as now, dope was a hugely profitable business. And who was the head of the drug ring in Terre Haute? Frank "Buster" Clark, of course.

Buster had connections with big suppliers in Detroit and St. Louis. The wholesale price of heroin at the end of World War I was about $111 per ounce, while cocaine sold for $14. Clark, being such a big distributor, was able to buy his heroin for $85 per ounce and cocaine for $1.25, though if they were running short between supplies, he would have to buy his stock from bootleggers at a higher price.

The drugs were cut into "shots," which were one-quarter of a grain. Since there were over 400 grains per ounce, it made a tidy profit. Buster was clearing $1,700 per ounce after all his expenses. The feds were watching him. When one of his mules, a black man named "Bubbles" Haynes, was caught with heroin tied between his shoulders during a trip back from St. Louis, Clark was in trouble.

The federal agents paid Clark and his wife, Lottie, a visit at their "soft drink parlor." With the advent of Prohibition, many saloons were suddenly converted into soft drink parlors. So, Buster's place sold soft drinks with a little booze on the side. When the agents walked through the door, they were not looking for a bottle of Coca-Cola. They went straight to a safe and found a five-pound can of opium.

Clark was tried as a drug ringleader in federal court in 1920. At first, he was not too worried. He told a reporter that he always knew how previous indictments would "come out." However, they had cost him "big money" for lawyers, and he was almost broke. Then, sounding like a child, he whined he was tired of everyone picking on him.

His instinct was to plead not guilty as he had done in the past. However, his lawyer pointed out that this was a federal court and advised him to enter a guilty plea. Clark decided to plead out on the case, thinking all his political contacts would get him out of the charges. At worst, he thought he would get six months of prison time. He almost collapsed when the judge ordered him to serve four years in the federal penitentiary in Atlanta.

The cell door had barely shut behind him when his political friends began petitioning for his release. They were unsuccessful at first, but his friends in

The "Vice Squad"—including Buster Clark (*seated in car*) and Eddie Gosnell (*in hat, leaning on car fender*). *Bob Ferguson Collection.*

higher offices, including a congressman, eventually got him released in time for Christmas 1921.

The Terre Haute Buster Clark returned to was a different and much more violent world. There had always been occasional murders and infighting among the Terre Haute underworld, but it was nothing like the violence that would bloody the streets during Prohibition and the rise of gangs.

Clark quickly resumed his partnerships with Eddie Gosnell and Frank Meharry, Clark's brother-in-law. The group added bootlegging to their activities. They arranged for homemade booze and brought it in from the outside, which sometimes led to big trouble.

It did not take long for Clark to shift into high gear. Within months, he was the primary supplier of illegal booze in the Terre Haute area. When the feds dropped in to check out his roadhouse, they found 150 gallons of grain alcohol and $3,000 in cash. Once again, he was on their radar.

This was not supposed to happen in Terre Haute. Ora Davis, the new mayor, had declared—like so many mayors before him—that he was going to clean up the city and put a lid on prostitution, gambling and bootlegging. Someone from Terre Haute told an Indianapolis reporter it would not last long. He predicted that a prominent Republican politician known as Buster Clark's patron saint (he was likely speaking of John

Jensen, chairman of the Vigo County Republicans) would put pressure on Davis, and all would go back to normal. The informant must have been a seer, as he was right.

So, Frank "Buster" Clark carried on as before, but he would soon be battling new competition. In 1925, members of a local gang that included Pat Hageman and Charles Jenkins hijacked a carload of booze near the Wabash River Bridge. Not content with that plunder, they hatched another plot. A few days later, they crept up on a house on Third Avenue in Terre Haute. It belonged to Grover Vance, a partner of Clark's in a roadhouse. The gang broke into the house and kidnapped Vance and took him to their hideout. The guns staring Vance in his face convinced him that he best do as he was told. He picked up the phone and called Clark's booze supplier in St. Louis. He told them that Buster needed an emergency supply of booze right away. Soon, the shipment was on its way. Hageman's men were waiting for it in Terre Haute and hijacked the cargo of booze.

This, quite naturally, was looked upon with disfavor by the boys in St. Louis. They sent several emissaries armed with tommy guns and other instruments of reprisal to Terre Haute. The emissaries settled in a hotel and went out looking for Hageman and Jenkins. Luckily for the hijackers, they were soon ensconced in the rough surroundings of the Terre Haute hoosegow and out of the reach of the St. Louis triggermen. With no one to shoot, the St. Louisans returned home. It would not be their last trip to Terre Haute.

Cartoon lampooning efforts to clean up the West End. *Vigo County Historical Society.*

Clark and his wife liked to get away to their country home on Paris Avenue just beyond West Terre Haute. It was a place where they could relax and get away from the tumultuous times in Terre Haute. On the night of July 25, 1926, some fellows decided that Clark's windows would be ideal for target practice and riddled the house with bullets. Luckily, Clark and his family were not at home. They had already moved back to Terre Haute after a warning that they might be targeted. Clark told reporters, "I wouldn't be here today if I was in that house."

None of the shooters were identified, but Clark's partner Eddie Gosnell was later paid a similar visit by Al Capone and some of his boys.

The feds continued to keep an eye on Terre Haute and Buster Clark. In February 1927, they conducted their biggest raid in over a year. Clark and Frank Meharry were busted for a gambling den at their roadhouse on First Street. The next year, the pair were caught with forty-three gallons of booze. In an effort to keep Buster out of jail, his wife went to the sheriff to claim that the booze was actually hers and not Clark's. This didn't work, and Frank went to jail. In a "how the mighty have fallen" comment, one newspaper noted that Clark was once a "political power in the old saloon days."

Clark and the others involved in that raid were federal prisoners but were kept in the Vigo County Jail. They were given special privileges by Sheriff Ray Foncannon and would testify to that three years later in the federal trials dealing with corruption and the liquor ring.

Clark's last real time in the spotlight came during those 1930 trials. Many could not believe it, but he became a government witness during a grand jury investigation into political corruption in Terre Haute. It should not have come, since it was said that Clark was one of the first to turn on Donn Roberts in the 1915 fraud cases.

At the 1930 trial, Clark and his sister Dot testified that he stopped his bootlegging operations whenever he got tipped off to a raid thanks to Republican county chairman John Jensen. When Jensen gave the all-clear, they pulled out the booze again.

With the end of Prohibition, bootlegging died down, so one of Clark's slices of the pie went away. He maintained his gambling operations either alone or in partnership with Gosnell. He was growing older. He had led a tough life and had been the man in the riotous era that was the golden age of the West End.

He died in 1936—the same year as former mayor Donn Roberts—at age sixty-two.

THE QUEEN AND CROWN PRINCE OF VICE

Nobody could say that Edith Brown did not have brains and style. She went from a small farm near Paris, Illinois, to running the classiest, most famous brothel in Terre Haute.

When she made that trip to Terre Haute is not known, but she took a job as a housemaid for a wealthy family. But toiling as a maid for as little as three dollars per week was not enough for Edith. She wanted more out of life. She had in mind setting up a top-flight brothel furnished with style and open only to the best clientele. To make this dream a reality, she would need a little help. Along the way, she made the acquaintance of the owner of a furniture store. He provided just the help she needed. The man, a lifelong bachelor, became her "companion." He reportedly helped fund her brothels and provided the elegant furnishings for which her house would become known. He also offered her financial advice. Edith was a fast learner and bought premium stocks, like Standard Oil, that added to her wealth.

She hired her staff and set up business in 1899 or 1900. Her first house was at 211 N. First Street. When the 1900 census worker came to her house, she told him she was single, the head of the house and gave her profession as "sporting." Sporting was a period term for those involved in vice, like gamblers, prostitutes or madams. She was twenty-four years old and had two other young women living in the house, Catherine, age twenty-one, and Jennie, age eighteen. On her block and the next one, there were eleven brothels and forty-five prostitutes. Initially, she was just one of many madams in the West End, but she would later make her mark.

Madam Edith Brown in classic pose, circa 1920. *Vigo County Historical Society.*

Around 1901, she opened a brothel in a larger, two-story brick house at 213 Mulberry Street. Soon after, she hired a young man named Eddie Gosnell as a bouncer. Gosnell told a friend that he met Edith while trying to sell her insurance. Whether it was regular insurance or for protection is unknown. Gosnell was young, but he already knew his way around the West End. He was also working with the "King of the Levee," as Buster Clark was then known. Gosnell and Clark would be partners until Clark's death in 1936. Gosnell liked gambling and was an up-and-comer among the betting set. His stature would grow along with that of Edith Brown.

Edith Brown was always looking to improve, and she moved to an even nicer house at 318 Eagle Street in 1906. Finally, in 1917, she moved to what would be the palace among Terre Haute brothels. The two-story, sixteen-room building at 206 N. Second Street was previously owned by Buster Clark. Unusual for the period, it had three full bathrooms. A new (or possibly old) swain was to help her furnish it in ostentatious style. A prominent, married Terre Haute furniture owner was smitten with Edith, and he made sure she had luxurious surroundings. People marveled at the house with Oriental rugs, the best china and silver and ornate furniture.

Downstairs was Madam Brown's private sitting room, a music room with a grand piano, a sitting room, a living room, a dining room and a spectacular bar. The bar itself was from the Prairie House, once Terre Haute's finest hotel. A mirror dominated the back wall of the bar room. It was eight feet tall and twelve feet long with a gold-leaf frame. Whether it was true or not, the mirror was touted as being the world's largest one-piece mirror. It was said it was made in France and had originally been part of the 1893 World's Columbian Exposition in Chicago.

Madam Edith Brown's staff in front of her second brothel at 213 Mulberry Street, circa 1909. *Bob Ferguson Collection.*

Madam Edith Brown's brothel "palace." *Vigo County Historical Society.*

Visitors entering through the wrought-iron fence passed through a door adorned with a Tiffany canopy and also might have noted the formal garden. It was an elegant house that often catered to a wealthy clientele.

Though her house was classically furnished, Brown was also very modern. She drove one of the first electric cars, and the brothel was thought to be the first place in Terre Haute to have the newfangled invention known as a radio. She also installed Terre Haute's first private pool in the fenced backyard.

For centuries, a red light in the window was the way brothels advertised themselves. It was a bit too old-fashioned for Edith Brown. She started the trend of replacing the red light with a neon sign giving the street address.

While Brown was becoming the madam with the most, Eddie Gosnell was becoming a force in his own right. Perhaps descended from the second family to live in Terre Haute, he was the son of a riverboat captain. His father was also an inventor who received a patent for a grappling device in 1883.

Gosnell's early life is a bit mysterious. He worked on the railroad for a while, but his keen sense about gambling was what made him real money. His partnership with Buster Clark and his penchant for running gambling operations made him a big part of the "vice trust." Like Clark, he was indicted for his key role in the "Great Slot Machine Caper" but was not convicted.

Gosnell became more of his own man while Clark was in federal prison for dealing drugs. They remained partners after Clark's release in 1921, but there was a sense that Gosnell might be surpassing his criminal mentor. As Clark grew older, Gosnell carried much of the load of the partnership. He became heavily involved in bootlegging and opened the first of a string of roadhouses and gambling dens.

Gosnell married Edith Brown in 1924 while they were vacationing in Hot Springs, Arkansas, another sin city. They took a trip with friends throughout the West and camped in the Grand Canyon. They returned to Terre Haute, but, oddly, would never live together full-time. Gosnell continued to live simply in an apartment at his Rod and Gun Club, while Edith stayed at her house. Gosnell had special ladies' nights on Thursdays. Each Thursday, Edith Brown came to the club, spent the night and returned to her house early Friday morning.

They were the royal couple of Terre Haute vice.

Gosnell was a tough man, hot-tempered but fair. He told a bodyguard that he made a lot of enemies in his life. Once his people proved themselves to him, Gosnell would always look after them. A young man named Newton was Gosnell's driver during Prohibition. Seeing all the money being made, he told Gosnell that he wanted to quit and become a bootlegger. Gosnell told him that he did not think the young man had what it took to survive in that cutthroat world. He was worried he would be killed but let him go, saying he could always come back to his old job if things didn't work out. Still worried about his protégé, Gosnell was sure he would be killed in a bootleg war. Gosnell had him arrested in Evansville while carrying a load of whiskey. Newton spent nine months in the Evansville jail, but he was alive. He went back to work for Gosnell upon his release.

Gosnell did not become involved with Joe Traum and his St. Louis gang. He considered them big fish in a small pond. While the Traums allied themselves with Al Capone, Gosnell went his own way. He supplied booze to "Bugs" Moran, Capone's archenemy in Chicago (Capone was likely responsible for the Valentine's Day Massacre of seven of Moran's gang in 1929). That did not sit well with Scarface.

One day, Capone and five of his gang decided to pay Eddie a visit. They knocked on the door of the Rod and Gun Club. When the black housekeeper, who was with Gosnell for fifty years, opened the door, she found a pistol staring her in the face. Capone told her to get Eddie. So frightened she urinated on herself, she told him that Eddie was not there. Capone pointed to Eddie's Cadillac (Gosnell always had two Caddies—one new, the other a year old) and said he must be here. She explained he had two and wasn't there. After telling her to let Eddie know he was looking for him, Capone then led his men away. He did not know that Gosnell never lived at the club, though his staff had rooms there. He actually lived in an apartment over the garage. From there, Gosnell watched Capone. He had an array of guns in front of him and planned to kill them all if they discovered his apartment. Also in the apartment was a ring that belonged to Moran. Eddie had purchased it for $500 from Arthur Zamberletti, who needed money and was about to enter Leavenworth.

Despite being a gangster who had killed at least two men, there was a Robin Hood side to Gosnell. He had his own set of ethics. Married men were not allowed to appear in public at his clubs with a girlfriend. Gosnell did not wish their wives to be embarrassed if it became known. Having come from a poor background, he looked out for the poor in Terre Haute. Each year, he went to Henry Smith, owner of the Deep Vein Mining Company, and purchased four or five carloads of coal. They would then be left on sidings around town. Eddie would then let it be known that those who needed fuel for the winter could help themselves but take just what they needed and leave the rest for others.

An example of how Gosnell could separate his business and personal lives so completely was found in the activities he allowed at his Oak View roadhouse. The Oak View Club consisted of two buildings, the clubhouse and the auditorium. Even though he loved dogs, he offered the twin barbarities of cockfighting and dogfighting in the auditorium and collected bets on the fights. He and his wife, Edith Brown, both adored dogs—she liked pugs, while Gosnell was partial to spaniels. Edith even buried her dogs in her back garden, each with its own headstone to mark its importance in her life. Despite that, Gosnell still offered the dogfights. Whether Edith was aware of this side of Eddie's business is unknown. She probably was not.

Gambling was Gosnell's true love. Each of his businesses, from the 12 Points Hotel to the Rod and Gun Club, featured gambling. His game was roulette. He loved boxing and horses. He promoted professional boxing in the Terre Haute area and often trained his fighters himself. For years, he kept a stable in the West End, and there were always horses at the farm at the Rod and Gun Club. When a thirty-year-old racehorse kept at the farm died, Gosnell told Bob Ferguson to bury the old steed. Ferguson spent hours digging by hand and with a tractor. When he thought he had dug deep enough, he used the tractor to bury the horse. It just so happened that the horse fell into the grave feet-up. Ferguson started filling in the grave. He had not dug it deep enough. When he finished, all four of the hooves were sticking out above the ground. It became a sight to see.

Edith Brown was probably the most well-known woman in Terre Haute during her time. She was something of a celebrity. She was not shunned—at least not to her face. After all, some of the wealthiest and most powerful men in the city were regular visitors at her house. She and a "companion" regularly dined at the finest restaurants and attended theater and social events. She did not even pretend that she was ashamed of the life she chose. She was a proud woman. She was generous with donations to many Terre Haute causes, particularly those benefitting children.

Her furniture-baron friend often stopped by the brothel. In July 1929, he entered the house in a bad mood. He made the mistake of arguing with Brown in view of others. He made the ultimate mistake by slapping her while Eddie Gosnell was in the room. The hot-tempered Gosnell could not be contained. He rushed on the man and beat him senseless. The bloodied man was taken home. He died a few days later at St. Anthony Hospital. The cause of death was listed as auto intoxication, which was caused by toxins released within the body. It could be caused by many things, such as blows to the lower body.

Brown continued to operate the best little whorehouse in Terre Haute. Her moneyed guests were entertained by live music and sipped the best liquor, even during Prohibition. She hosted elegant parties on many Sundays. The guests sometimes included the wives of prominent men. Everyone was required to wear formal dress. Not all the male visitors partook of *all* of the pleasures of the house. Many just stopped by for the elegant surroundings or for interesting conversations. Among them was Terre Haute businessman and poet Max Ehrmann, writer of *Desiderata*.

A man who grew up in the West End recalled chauffeur-driven cars cruising to the back of the house. They dropped off men headed to Brown's little pleasure dome, but their identities were hidden from view by latticework screens. They were also assured of privacy by the madam. In some houses, groups of men gathered together in a parlor while girls were paraded in front of them—not at Madam Brown's. Each visitor was ushered into a private room, where they could make their choice unseen by others.

The women they chose from were beautiful. Brown made sure they were elegantly dressed, and they sometimes wore evening gowns. Even when they went out, they had to be nicely dressed. A man recalled them coming into his father's grocery store, and they were all sedately dressed. From their demeanor and clothing, one never would have guessed their profession. They were good customers who paid in cash. Since they were allowed to have pets, some of them had the butcher grind round steak for their dogs.

Madam Brown's girls were always "safe." She made them register both their real names and "brothel" names with the health department and be given a clean bill of health before she hired them. All prostitutes were supposed to be checked at least monthly, but some of the sleazier brothels ignored this dictum. The prostitutes were a bit coddled in the good houses. They were expected to keep their own rooms, but maids were available. Brown's domestic staff included several maids, a cook and gardener-handymen. For all this, the girls had to follow the rules, be polite and maintain a sense of decorum.

For all of these reasons, Madam Brown's house set the standard. During the heyday of the West End, it was likely that the other brothels were two- to five-dollar houses, but Brown's women were easily able to command double or triple that rate—or more.

Madam Brown's house was very well known. Actors, musicians and gangsters, like Capone and Dillinger, made stops at her house. Perhaps the best illustration came by way of a sailor from Terre Haute. He was stationed at a naval base in Panama during World War II when he started talking to a shipmate. His mate asked him where he was from, and he told him Terre Haute, Indiana. The first words out of his fellow sailor's mouth were, "Oh, Madam Brown."

When most of the West End was closed down during World War II because of a naval training program at Indiana State University and concerns about military men passing through town, Madam Brown closed the house. After over four decades in the business, she quit. She turned the house into a hotel for men. However, she may have kept her hand in her old business in a minor way for a short period after the war. Eddie Gosnell once sent one of his men to the Filbeck Hotel in downtown Terre Haute to pick up two girls and take them to Edith's. When he asked how he would recognize them, Eddie told the man they were waiting for him, and he would know them when he saw them. He did.

With the end of Prohibition and bootlegging, Gosnell concentrated on his gambling operations. He devoted his time to the Rod and Gun Club, where the roulette wheel spun and spun. He enjoyed acting as croupier.

Edith Brown moved to Florida in 1954 and into a house Eddie had built for them. Eddie often vacationed with her. Gosnell died in Florida in 1961.

Before he left, he told Bob Ferguson to look after things, as he would not return to Terre Haute. His end was near. When Ferguson replied that he was fine and said Eddie would be back before he knew it, Eddie said he knew he was going to die there. The ever-loyal Ferguson did as he was asked. He particularly looked out for Gosnell's beloved nephew Hobart, who was an alcoholic and prone to getting into fights. Ferguson eventually bought Gosnell's estate. His wife, Edith Brown, who had retired to Florida, preceded him in death. She died in Sarasota, Florida, at the age of 82 in 1956. Both she and Eddie had long and colorful lives.

A GANGSTER NAMED BOOBIE

*Y*ou can't place all the blame on Boobie Clark for making John Dillinger a gangster, but he certainly played his part.

Russell "Boobie" Clark (no relation to Buster Clark) was born in 1898. His place of birth has been disputed, but census records indicate he was born in Illinois. Little is known of his early life, but it is not difficult to imagine he was more than a bit wild. He joined the Marines during World War I, but Marine discipline and Boobie Clark were not a match. Clark was dishonorably discharged in 1919.

He soon gravitated toward Terre Haute, where he took up with gangster "Blackie" Linton. Blackie was known as a daring bank robber, and Boobie obviously learned a lot from the veteran criminal. Clark would later be known for his prowess at planning bank robberies. He was an expert at casing banks and devising intricate plans down to the minute.

During the early years of Prohibition, Clark began to rob the illegal roadhouses around the Terre Haute area. He knew it was a safe bet that the owners would not report the thefts to the police. Year after year, he dove deeper into the underworld. He became involved in the rampant bootlegging during Prohibition. In August 1926, Clark and fellow hood Jackie Morrison were suspected of kidnapping two bootleggers from the streets of West Terre Haute. "Shorty" Moore and Alek LeClerq were well known for their finesse with stills. They were good suppliers. Moore and LeClerq were released the next day but remained mum about the kidnapping. They understood that silence was not only golden but the key to their survival. They were

Boobie Clark state prison mugshot, 1926. *Indiana Archives and Records Administration.*

working for a St. Louis gang trying to muscle its way into the Terre Haute bootlegging operation; the kidnapping was meant to put a scare into them and make them back off.

Moore and LeClerq were lucky they did not suffer the fate of Danville, Illinois club owner Joe Popolardo. Clark and Morrison were believed to have murdered Popolardo in June 1926. Again, it was a dispute over territory, as someone was not pleased that Popolardo was distributing beer from a Cicero brewery. Cicero was Al Capone's territory.

Perhaps because he was feeling the heat, Boobie Clark left the area. He began a series of bank robberies in Northeast Indiana. He was caught after robbing a bank in tiny Huntertown, near Fort Wayne, in October 1927. Justice was swift, and by November, Boobie Clark had been sentenced to twenty-five years at the Indiana State Penitentiary at Michigan City. And there began a tale.

Clark soon befriended a young prisoner from Mooresville, Indiana. Suffering from gonorrhea and growing increasingly bitter, John Dillinger had decided that cops and the world were allied against him. So he said to hell with useful trades, though he was an adept shirt-maker in prison. Dillinger did not plan to live by anyone's rules but his own once he was released. He soon became the ardent pupil of Clark, Charley Makley,

Harry Pierpont and Homer Van Meter. All were veteran bank robbers, and Dillinger sat at the feet of the masters, soaking up all they could tell him about the intricacies of robbing banks and other criminal endeavors. Though he was younger and less experienced, he was a leader. That would later be made clear.

On the fringe of the group was another young man from Terre Haute. Ed Shouse, convicted of robbing a Terre Haute theater, would later be key in bringing down Boobie Clark and other Dillinger gang members.

Dillinger was paroled in May 1933, partly due to his father gathering signatures on a petition seeking the release of his son. Dillinger did not forget the mentors he left behind. His thoughts immediately turned to breaking them out of the state pen. He did just that on September 20, 1933. Using guns provided by Dillinger, Clark and nine other prisoners, including Makley, Pierpont and Shouse, broke out of the joint.

The jailbreak was well planned. They used the guns to capture guards as shields and calmly walked out the front gate. A small-town sheriff was unlucky enough to be in the wrong place at the wrong time. He was sitting in his car when the prison break occurred. Four of the escapees commandeered the car and used the sheriff as a hostage. They were soon caught, with one being killed, but the others were more successful.

The other six, including Clark, Pierpont, Makley and Shouse, sprinted across the street and stole a vehicle from a gas station. They made their way to Indianapolis, where Dillinger had arranged for them to have clothes, guns and cars waiting for them.

Clark and others went to a hideout in Terre Haute. Always planning ahead, Dillinger had earlier given $27,000 to a Kokomo madam to arrange the purchase of a house in Terre Haute. The gang hid out at the house on Fenwood Avenue. They did not stay long. On September 29, they stole a car near downtown Terre Haute and headed to Ohio, where Dillinger had been arrested. The gang robbed a bank in St. Marys, Ohio, to finance Dillinger's escape from the Lima Jail. On October 26, Clark, Pierpont, Shouse, Hamilton and Makley went to Lima.

In a plan likely devised by Clark, he, Pierpont and Makley entered the jail. Shouse was the lookout, and Hamilton guarded the getaway cars. Clark thought of everything. Posing as marshals, they strolled into the jailhouse, telling Sheriff Jess Sarber they were sent to escort Dillinger back to prison in Michigan City. When Sarber asked for credentials, Pierpont shot and killed him. Clark's gun accidently fired and nicked one of his own fingers. Hearing the shot, Dillinger calmly reached for his coat and waited for the gang to spring him. They were soon on their way.

Thus the original Dillinger gang was born. The three-month series of raids and bank robberies they committed made Dillinger infamous. The biggest heist was at a bank in Greencastle, Indiana. It is likely that Clark was the man who surveyed the bank, which included drawing up a floor plan of the bank and studying escape routes. On October 23, the gang hit the bank for a huge haul of $75,000 before escaping. Clark took part in at least two more robberies, in Racine and Chicago, with the gang.

Between robbery sprees, many of the gang hid out in Chicago, along with various girlfriends.

Clark called Opal Long his wife, though it is doubtful they were legally wed. Most of the other gangsters had pretty women on their arms. Opal could not match the other women for beauty. She was described as a big old girl. She was redheaded, nearsighted and freckled. She was also heavyset with enormous breasts and an ample behind. Behind her back, some of the others called her a "Mack truck," but she was the nicest and most caring of the women and was utterly devoted to Boobie Clark. She would later demonstrate just how devoted she was.

During their stay in Chicago, Russell "Boobie" Clark was named public enemy number five by the state of Illinois; Dillinger, of course, was ranked number one.

In November, a car carrying three men broke down just outside Indianapolis. They came upon a man named Paul Walton from Avon. They offered him five dollars to take them to Plainfield, then an additional fifteen dollars to chauffeur them to Terre Haute. Walton noticed they had a blanket wrapped around what looked like guns, but he needed the money he would get from this little trip. After directing Walton on a circuitous route to Terre Haute, they had him drop them off on the east side near 2531 Fenwood Avenue.

Boobie Clark's devoted girlfriend, Opal Long. *American University Library.*

It being late, Walton decided to stay in Terre Haute for the night. The following morning, his worried family called the police. When Walton finally returned home, he talked to the police about the men who were so anxious to get to Terre Haute. He also mentioned the rolled-up blanket. That aroused the suspicions of the police, who took Walton to look at mug shots. He identified Makley, Shouse and Harry Copeland from their mug shots. Immediately, word went out among law enforcement officials that they had a chance to nab some members of the Dillinger gang.

Roadblocks were set up, patrols increased and houses searched as state police, National Guardsmen and private and bank detectives hurried to Terre Haute. Finally, just before dawn on November 10, more than one hundred pursuers anxiously gathered outside the brown house at 2531 Fenwood Avenue. Excitement was high. Each man had thoughts about being able to proudly relate that he was part of the group that got Dillinger. Such boastful ideas quickly evaporated. When they pushed their way into the house, they learned the gangsters had gone. They had waited too long. Another chance lost. But at least one of gangsters would return to Terre Haute.

Some of the gang went to join Dillinger in Florida for a Christmas holiday. While they were cavorting around Daytona Beach, Ed Shouse was tracked to Paris, Illinois. As a state trooper named Teague moved in to capture Shouse, a fellow trooper tragically let loose with his riot gun, killing Teague. Shouse was taken back to Michigan City. Turning state's evidence, little Ed Shouse unraveled his tale. He told his inquisitors about the Sarber murder in Lima and also that Dillinger had attempted to combine Baby Face Nelson's gang with his. His plan was to use the combined forces, and Nelson's expertise, to rob the Dixie Flyer train in Terre Haute. The plan was later dropped.

The new year of 1934 was barely born when bank president Charles H. Ray found out that the Dillinger gang was casing his State Bank of West Terre Haute. The gang, being familiar with the area, saw the tiny bank as a juicy target. On Saturday, January 6, Ray was visited by Ivan Herring, West Terre Haute's town marshal. Evidently, Herring was more well-connected to the doings of the criminal element than most small-town marshals, for he had somehow gotten word that members of the Dillinger gang were going to rob the bank of its Monday payroll funds. Herring had a snitch, whose identity he would not reveal as it would mean a "ride" for the underworld tattletale.

Astounded and fearful, Ray contacted another banker named Howard Derry, who arranged for the bank president to meet with Terre Haute chief of police Armstrong. Word that the Dillinger gang was near became a call to action, and a plan was put in place.

It was decided that Ray would appear to pick up the funds from a bank in Terre Haute on Monday as usual. The Terre Haute police would follow surreptitiously and foil the robbery. Ray returned home to spend an anxious weekend waiting for Monday.

On Monday morning, January 8, Ray drove to the bank on Wabash Avenue, went inside and came back out with a dummy package of money. At about 8:30 a.m., Ray, dodging street cars, did a U-turn on Wabash Avenue and headed toward West Terre Haute. He felt reassured when he saw the Terre Haute police car in his mirror. The feeling was fleeting.

As he crossed the Wabash River Bridge, it all became too real for him. Waiting on the bridge was a Ford V8 (Dillinger's gang preferred high-powered cars like this or Hudson Terraplanes, usually stolen, as getaway cars) with Ohio license plates. It was exactly the type of car Herring had told them the robbers would be driving. At least two men (three men was considered the minimum for a successful bank robbery: one to be the getaway driver, one to be a lookout, one to do the actual robbery) were in the car. The car began to follow the nervous banker.

As Ray drove over the grade, he looked back one more time. To his astonishment, instead of following behind both cars, the Terre Haute police car sped up and insinuated itself between the bank president's car and the robbers' car. He "wondered why they [Terre Haute police] didn't drop back, but supposed it was part of the plan."

Bewildered, Ray drove on to his bank on Paris Avenue. He parked, looked around and hurried into the bank with his dummy package. When nothing happened, Ray went out to the police car parked next to the bank.

Leaning into the window, he nervously asked the policemen what had happened to the car with Ohio plates. Looking confused, the police said they didn't know but would try to find it. They had been sent out with no instructions. "It was awful."

Finally, the police said they would attempt to find the robbers and sped off. Herring, submachine gun in hand, led the search, which included knocking on the door of the Frey family on Larimer Hill and asking if Dillinger was there. They thought they were in luck when they spotted the car parked by the clay plant on the western edge of town. But as they approached, tommy guns were thrust out of the window as a warning, and the car began to hurtle along the National Road to Illinois. The police car, they said, got "snarled in traffic." As the chances of a traffic jam in West Terre Haute were somewhere between slim and none, it must be assumed that this was just an excuse. Yet another chance was lost.

Ray and the police then tried to figure out what had gone wrong. Again, they said they did not have instructions about exactly how to foil the robbery plot. Three robbers had been in the car. Dillinger and Clark were not among them, but they identified known gang members named Burke and Burt. Evidently, hiding on the floor of the backseat along with his trusty tommy gun, was Charles Makley.

Makley, known as Fat Charley, had spent Christmas in Florida with Dillinger at a gang hideout. They had a merry Christmas and exchanged gifts like jewelry and a puppy for Dillinger's girlfriend. Makley then decided to head back. Maybe he thought robbing a small bank along the way would break up the trip nicely. After the failed robbery in West Terre Haute, Makley and the other gangsters continued west to a gang hideout in Arizona.

That Monday night, Charles Ray noted in his diary that, "Ivan knew the story. Our plan was perfect, but because police headquarters didn't give the squad they sent out any information they missed a great chance" to capture some of the Dillinger gang.

One must wonder if the failure was due to ineptness or a tip from an informant in the Terre Haute police that warned the gang of what might happen. Either, or both, were possibilities, as corruption was a constant in the Terre Haute police department.

The fear of robbery continued. For weeks after the Dillinger gang scare, Charles Ray had a police escort from the time he picked up the payroll in Terre Haute until he safely reached the bank in West Terre Haute. On at least one occasion, Ivan Herring planted himself in the back room of the bank with a shotgun in his hands and a Springfield at his side. Luckily, he did not have to use them.

Makley continued heading west to Tucson. He would later be joined by Clark and others. Arizona was a nice, warm place to hide out for the winter. Were it not for a fire, the history of John Dillinger and his gang would have been quite different.

The gang had as many as four houses in Tucson to use as hideouts, but Boobie Clark and Charley Makley were staying at the Congress Hotel in late January. One evening, a fire broke out at the hotel. Clark and Makley gave two firemen fifty dollars to rescue two valuable trunks from their rooms. Upon chance does fate turn. The next day, one of the firemen was casually reading a detective magazine at the fire station. He recognized Makley's face staring up at him from the page. He called the police.

Whether it was confusion caused by the fire or simply hubris, Makley had stupidly given his home address to the firemen. The police quickly

Boobie Clark (*in bandage*) and John Dillinger (*top left*) after capture in Arizona. Yuma Sun.

staked out the house. When they saw Clark, Opal Long and Harry Pierpont and his girlfriend join Makley, they rushed the house. While the gang scrambled to get away as police entered the house, Opal slammed the door, breaking an officer's hand. It was not enough. Police arrested the gangsters. At the jail, the apparently unfrisked Pierpont pulled two pistols and tried to shoot his way out, but he was subdued.

Dillinger and his girlfriend arrived in Tucson unaware that members of his gang had been captured. After getting no answer to his knock on Boobie Clark's door, he turned to come face to face with police. The Tucson police had done what others could not.

Dillinger, commenting on Clark and Makley paying the firemen such a big reward, said, "If the saps had made it only a couple of bucks, we'd still be safe and happy."

The entire gang was returned to Ohio.

On March 22, Ed Shouse was brought from Michigan City to Lima for the trials of Makley, Pierpont and Clark. Shouse testified that Pierpont was the killer. He refused to testify against Makley at his trial and later told the court that Clark was not the trigger man. Pierpont and Makley were convicted of murder and sentenced to death by electric chair.

While Clark stoically sat through his trial, Opal Long continued to support him. She went to Dillinger's favorite lawyer in Chicago and gave him all the money she had to go to Lima and represent Clark. It did little good. Russell "Boobie" Clark was sentenced to life in prison. Opal continued to try to help him. She approached Dillinger several times seeking money to fund an appeal for Clark. Dillinger grew tired of her pestering and stopped seeing her.

Clark spent the next thirty-four years in prison. He was released for health reasons in 1968 and went to live with his sister in Detroit.

Russell "Boobie" Clark died on Christmas Eve in 1968.

OUR GANGS

Prohibition was an ill-conceived, benighted, stupid and foolhardy attempt at social engineering. Foisted upon the majority by an often honestly concerned but also holier-than-thou vocal minority, it was not only an abject failure but a disaster for the nation. It had terrible consequences for the United States during its tenure (from 1920 to 1933) and long after.

During Prohibition, bootleggers—the term is thought to originate from the days when sailors would hide contraband in their tall boots to spirit a little comfort onto their ships for the long sea journey, or, perhaps, from Civil War soldiers carrying booze in their boots—cropped up everywhere. There were an estimated 200 stills, large and small, operating in the Terre Haute area during most of Prohibition. To some bootleggers, it was akin to printing money, so large were the profits. Bootleg liquor and beer were easy to make. All you needed were easy-to-find ingredients and patience.

Malt syrup was the main ingredient needed for making beer. It could be purchased in most grocery stores. When a band of frustrated, hungry people broke into a Kroger store in West Terre Haute in 1934, they not only made off with milk, bread and meat but emptied the store of tins of malt syrup. The ubiquitous and infamous "bathtub gin" made during Prohibition was created using denatured alcohol, like rubbing alcohol or mineral spirits. It was diluted with a little water and lemon or apple peels and left to "distill." A few days to a week later, and voilà, you had gin. It was nasty stuff and had to be mixed with some type of juice to make it even close to palatable, but it was guzzled by those in need of an alcoholic drink.

Moonshine, white mule and other types of homemade whiskey took a little longer to make but were not that difficult to distill. Because grain alcohol was cheaper than distilled alcohol, it formed the base of most bootleg liquor. Grocery stores could provide moonshiners with the needed corn syrup or sugar, yeast and other ingredients.

And if you liked wine, all you needed was access to grapes and indifference to having purple feet.

It should be noted that one aspect of Prohibition is often misunderstood. The manufacturing and selling of alcohol was against the law, but drinking it was not.

Of course, not all illegal liquor manufactured during Prohibition was homemade. Eddie Gosnell made several trips to Cuba and Puerto Rico to arrange shipments of rum, thus the term "rumrunner" for those who brought real liquor into the country. An even bigger source was Canada, home to many breweries and distilleries and a porous border. Canadian booze was boated to the East Coast and off-loaded onto smaller, faster boats. Internally, rumrunners used the Great Lakes to ship liquor south.

Terre Haute had an additional valuable resource. It was the home of a major distillery and brewery until the advent of Prohibition. Many of those who lost their jobs at the brewery used their skills to make alcohol for themselves or to sell or were hired by bootleggers to make product.

A major reason Prohibition was a disaster was the role it played in the rise of organized crime. Yes, there were loosely organized gangs throughout the United States before Prohibition, but they were local. In Terre Haute, the underworld was a local affair essentially run by Frank "Buster" Clark. Prohibition brought a new and more dangerous underworld element to the area. Terre Haute was only 169 miles from St. Louis and 179 miles from Chicago. With the huge profits that could be made by bootlegging, it was natural for the big-city gangsters to expand to other areas. Both cities looked to Terre Haute as prime territory, but the St. Louis boys were most successful in infiltrating gangs here.

Instead of trying to muscle Terre Haute crime figures like Clark and Eddie Gosnell out of business, the St. Louis gang formed loose, ever-changing partnerships with characters in the local underworld.

The dominant figures from St. Louis were Joe Traum and his brother Jake "Blackie" Traum. Joe was called the "most wanted, but least convicted" gangster in Terre Haute. They said they were part of the Egan Rats gang from St. Louis. Whether there really was such a gang or if the Traums gave themselves the moniker is unknown. Joe Traum later told a famous Hautean madam that they had just made up the name to frighten people. Also in doubt was whether Traum was "officially" sent as an emissary of St. Louis gangs or came on his own. No matter the truth, the Traums and their Missouri brethren considerably ratcheted up the violence around Terre Haute during their reign.

If a police drama were set in Terre Haute during this time, one might see a bulletin board set up in the detective squad room. On that board, a picture of Joe Traum would be at the center, and from it would stretch a spiderweb of lines running to other gangsters. This would be the Terre Haute version of a "most wanted" list.

A Hautean Rogues' Gallery

Ralston "Blackie" Linton was born in Mississippi and became a pretty good bank robber after moving to Terre Haute. On November 6, 1923, he and a gang pulled off spectacular bank robberies in Spencer, Indiana. With a carload of accomplices, he executed a well-planned heist. Lookouts were posted on street corners as Linton cut the lights and phone lines in the banks. The take from the robberies was $17,000. On their way out, the gang was spotted, and gunfire raked the streets. Three locals were wounded as the gang escaped.

Linton and four of the gang, including William Highfield, were arrested in a Terre Haute roadhouse in May 1924. They were sent to the Owen County Jail in Spencer. It was not the most secure jail in the state. That December, Linton and Highfield sawed their way out of the jail. It seems they were left alone at the jail when the sheriff and his deputies stepped out. They may have gotten the saws when Highfield's wife and kids visited him. His wife was searched, but the children were not; they might have slipped daddy a saw or two. Linton and Highfield rushed out of jail, hopped into a high-powered car and sped west and out of Spencer.

Linton surrendered to police in Terre Haute in January 1925. In early April, he was sentenced to fifteen to twenty-five years in the state prison and sent back to the Spencer jail. Again, he escaped, this time with keys provided by his wife, Pearl. He was not on the loose for very long. A week later, he was captured in Clinton, Indiana, after more than fifty shots were fired. He was again returned to the Spencer jail, but this time he was under twenty-four-hour guard until he was taken to the state prison.

Meanwhile, his wife, Pearl, whom he had married in 1922, returned to running her Terre Haute roadhouse. It seems that Pearl got lonely with her husband away from their marital bed. In December 1926, there was a little party at the roadhouse when two men, Joe Donham and Ralph Henry, vied for Pearl's affection. A brawl broke out, with Pearl tossing dishes, Victrola records and furniture as her weapons of choice. When the police arrived, Pearl tried to stop them at the door. A deputy pushed his way in, and gunfire erupted. Fern House, wife of gangster Al Donham, and another hood named Fred Henry suffered mortal wounds. Pearl and the others were taken to jail. The incident was one of the reasons that Blackie and Pearl later divorced.

Homer Wright was a tough man. A madam who knew both Wright and Joe Traum well said that Wright was the only man who could make Traum jump. Traum was afraid of his one-time bodyguard. Wright was a top-rank rumrunner who could be counted on to pick up and deliver a load of illegal booze. But he was also arrested many times for bootlegging, gambling, bank robbery and other crimes. He served time in the Missouri state prison for armed robberies in the early 1920s and was arrested for fencing stolen jewelry in Chicago in 1927.

Known as the "King of Indiana Bootleggers," Arthur "Arturo" Zamberletti was a colorful character who was a bit full of himself. He liked to sport colorful smoking jackets as if he were Cary Grant, liked flashy cars and even owned an airplane. He started his vice career running a brothel in Clinton. His first bootleg operations included two fifty-gallon stills in Jasonville, Indiana, that produced white mule. When he was caught the first time, he had 150 gallons set to send out and an amazing total of 1,600 gallons of raisin mash ready to be used.

He often made bootlegging runs to Chicago with Eddie Gosnell. They loaded stripped-down Cadillacs with false panels to hide their cargo. On some trips, they led a convoy of a dozen or more Caddies carrying booze. A bit of counterfeiting was also undertaken by Arthur and his family. His mother, Anna, was arrested for using phony liquor stamps and bond labels in 1925 after hiding out in Illinois for two years.

Bootlegging was the thread that tied together most of the gang members, but some had sidelines. Jackie Bell was a gunman suspected or arrested in connection with several murders. Ed "Machine Gun" O'Hare was a hijacker and suspected of being one of the hitmen in the Valentine's Day Massacre. William Highfield did a little hijacking. Jack Morrison lent his hand to

Arthur Zamberletti (*seated*) and Eddie Gosnell alongside a Cadillac with hidden panels used to hide bootleg liquor. *Bob Ferguson Collection.*

armed robbery and kidnapping. He teamed with Boobie Clark, in his pre–Dillinger Gang days, to rob a club in Evansville and kidnap two West Terre Haute bootleggers.

Not all bootleggers were big-timers. Some were like Acle Ellingsworth, a quiet, unassuming man in West Terre Haute. Being a tinsmith, it was nothing for Ellingsworth to whip up a still in his shed and set about being a minor Jack Daniel. He was not a gangster. He made small batches of whiskey, mainly to sell or give to his neighbors or for his own consumption. He was not one who distilled great amounts to sell to rumrunners or supply a string of speakeasies, of which there were many in Vigo County. His daughter-in-law Eileen Ellingsworth remembered, "He never used any money he made bootlegging for himself. He would use it to help out neighbors or a family in need."

Looking back, John Lamb, a former executive secretary of the Terre Haute Chamber of Commerce, estimated that there were more than two hundred bootleggers in Terre Haute during Prohibition. Again, these were small-time operations in which beer or whiskey were made for personal use or to share with friends and family. Since many of these stills were located in basements, Lamb theorized that this may have changed Americans' view of those dingy downstairs rooms devoted to furnaces or storing canned goods. He believed that so many people became used to gathering there to drink illegal liquor that they began to wonder what it would be like if the basement was smartened up and turned into a sort of underground living room.

Bootlegging was the primary cash cow, but gambling, increased drug dealing and prostitution would help fill the gang leaders' coffers.

Fast Women, Faster Cars

Big-time bootleggers liked their fast women, and they also reveled in big, speedy cars. They tended to like big cars like Hudson Terraplanes, Duesenbergs, Packards and Cadillacs. John Dillinger preferred Duesenbergs and big Fords. Big cars allowed them to pack a lot of booze. Speed was essential for escaping other gangsters or police. And a great mechanic was essential.

Nelson Fortune was a former clay worker who had a garage at 110 E. Paris Avenue in West Terre Haute. He was a wizard with engines, and word got around that he was the guy to see. Gangsters began to roll into West Terre Haute looking for Fortune's garage. His grandson, also named Nelson, recalls playing around the garage. He would look into his grandfather's big rolltop desk, and in the cubbyholes, he would find invoices bearing names like Capone. Gangsters would roll into the garage and leave their cars for Fortune to give them a tune-up. The gangsters would then head to Terre Haute—often to the brothels in the West End—for a little relaxation and let the wizard do his work. There weren't many police or revenue agent cars that could keep up with Fortune's handiwork, and they became used to seeing taillights growing smaller ahead of them.

Life as a Gamble

Terre Haute had long been a haven for gamblers. They were everywhere. Like Eddie Gosnell, they knew what they were doing and how to fleece the unwary.

Mr. Levervitch was a former state senator from Sullivan, Illinois. After a disappointing 1910 election loss, he decided he deserved a rest. Like many in the Midwest, he went to the spa at French Lick. There, he took steams, had his body fluffed and folded by masseurs and relaxed in the evening with a drink.

One night, he made friends with an affable fellow named Jack Farney. They got on well, and Farney learned his new friend liked a bit of gambling. If that was the case, Farney told Levervitch, you need to meet my friend Rooney. It turned out that Rooney had devised a "cold deck" machine that guaranteed one could win at poker. A cold deck was one that had been tampered with so that it contained a preset series of good hands, but the winning hand would come to the dealer. By getting a good hand, the other gamblers thought they had a winner, so they would continue raising the stakes, but the dealer would actually have the winning hand and would rake in the big pot.

The problem was that Rooney was short of ready cash. Why Levervitch did not stop to wonder why Rooney was short of cash if he had a machine that guaranteed him a win can only be put down to greed. Levervitch said he would stake Rooney to the cash he needed. After the big wins, they would split the pot in half. They were ready to head out for their big score.

Both agreed that Terre Haute was "about the livest [sic] town in the middle west." What better place to find high rollers and "fleece the gambler's flocks"?

They jumped on a train heading to Terre Haute. They checked into the Great Northern hotel and spread the word that they were "live ones" looking for a big game. They were pointed to a place on Wabash Avenue. It was the haunt of big-time gamblers where the "limit is the ceiling above the table." It seemed perfect. Rooney was invited to join the big boys at the table.

As the pot grew, Rooney gave Levervitch the sign that he was going to use their secret weapon. Levervitch tried not to show his excitement. It looked like the new "sharks" in town were about to cheat their way into winning a mound of money. Just then, an "innocent bystander" opined that with stakes this high, maybe the deck should be cut before the final draw. This, of course, changed the order of the hands. Levervitch looked on in horror as Rooney lost the hand. Visions of glory and a $350 pot blew by the bewildered Levervitch.

It only took a moment for Levervitch to realize that he, not the Terre Haute rubes, had been played for a sucker. Rooney was their partner, not his. His roar that he had been cheated echoed through the room as those who were in on the plot tried to hide their gleeful smiles. Rooney, not wanting to lose a sucker who had been bitten hard on his hook, tried to calm Levervitch. It was just the luck of the draw, he said. They could still work this scam all across Illinois if they stayed together. Poorer but wiser, Levervitch spit out the hook and clomped out of the saloon, swearing under his breath all the way back to the hotel.

The next morning, Levervitch practically sprinted to the prosecutor's office. Barging into the office, he explained he was an important Illinois politician, had been cheated and wanted the crooks arrested. The prosecutor, used to such fulminations, told Levervitch he would have them arrested immediately if given their names. However, Levervitch would have to stay in town to testify.

Levervitch blanched and said he couldn't do that. The prosecutor would have to do it without him. "I can't afford to be known in such a disgraceful affair." That was no good, the prosecutor explained. It would be useless to file a complaint unless Levervitch signed an affidavit and remained in town until the trial to testify. The Illinois politician said that he must return to Sullivan to take care of some things first. He would return the next day to sign an affidavit.

Evidently, Levervitch decided his reputation was worth more to him than $350 and stayed in Illinois. It would not have been worth his time to return to the scene of the crime anyway. Fearing arrest, Rooney and his accomplices had skipped town while Levervitch was asleep at the Great Northern.

There were sub-gangs within the larger gangs, and each seemed to have their own specialties. Some liked robbing gas stations; the haul was smaller, but so were the dangers.

In January 1924, there was a series of seventeen gas station robberies in Terre Haute. There was no real pattern to the robberies, so police began to stake out stations in different parts of the city. Detective Steve Kendall was assigned to a Sho-Mo station on the north side on January 23, 1924. Two men drove into the station that evening and ordered two dollars of gas. One of the men, named Ed Barber, followed the attendant back inside to get change. He then pulled a gun and demanded the cash box. Detective Kendall, who was hiding in the bathroom, pulled out his gun and stepped into the room. Barber raised his gun, and he and Kendall simultaneously fired. Barber's aim was better. His bullet slammed into the detective's jaw. Kendall slumped to the floor as Barber jumped into the getaway car, and he and his partner sped away. Detective Kendall lay dying on the floor.

Barber and his partner, Joseph Parker, were later arrested, and their trial was assigned to neighboring Brazil. Both were convicted of robbery and murder. Barber, who was only seventeen years old, became the youngest person ever given the death penalty in Indiana. There were rumors that the

St. Louis boys were not going to let him be executed. One evening, there was a report of two carloads of hoods on the way to Brazil to break out Barber and Parker, who were quickly transferred to the more secure Terre Haute jail. Sure enough, there were sightings of two cars with Missouri plates cruising around Brazil. Police went out looking for them but lost them on the back roads. As for Barber and Parker? After a series of stays of execution, Barber's sentence was reduced to twenty-five years in prison. Parker got a new trial and was convicted of banditry and became eligible for parole in ten years.

Bert Tosser liked to steal other people's things. Tosser was a homegrown talent who began his felonious career before Prohibition. He was a doughy-faced man with a nose that appeared to have played host to a few too many fists. He started out stealing as a youngster and eventually came under the tutelage of Buster Clark. Tosser was involved with the great auto tires caper initiated by Clark and Eddie Gosnell in 1915. He also learned the ropes of election fraud from Clark.

During World War I, Tosser became part of the Pierman gang. That little gang was credited with $1 million of war bonds, war savings stamps and postage stamps. They also had a nice sideline in robbing banks.

Tosser moved around a bit and was arrested in Cincinnati for a series of burglaries. He was sentenced to the Ohio State Prison in Columbus but did not serve out his term. Tosser had friends in high places, it seems. Terre Haute mayor Charles Hunter and several city councilmen petitioned Ohio to release Tosser early. He had been back in Terre Haute for two months before the police knew he was home; evidently, Mayor Hunter had not bothered to inform them that a convicted felon was back on the streets.

By 1924, Tosser had taken up bank robbing. Along with two others, he drove to the bank in tiny Bridgeton, Indiana. They entered the bank, tied and gagged a teller and walked out with $1,400. Tosser was captured not by the police but by a private detective. His sentence was two to twenty-one years at the Indiana State Prison. Once again, political influence came to his rescue when Indiana governor Edward Jackson pardoned him in 1926.

While Tosser was away in prison, an incident occurred that proved he came by his dishonesty honestly. His sixty-eight-year-old mother, Sarah, was busted for running her own little bootlegging operation. When her home was raided, police found five hundred bottles of home brew, fifty more gallons of home brew cooking and hundreds of empty bottles. His brother Clifford was serving time as part of the Blackie Linton gang that robbed the Spencer banks.

Tosser had a half-interest in a cigar store on Wabash Avenue. Thinking it a good business plan to cater to two bad habits, the cigar store not only sold tobacco but gave its customers the option of washing it down with some beer or whiskey. That plan went awry when Tosser was busted along with others, including Buster Clark, in a federal raid on booze sellers. He spent six months as a federal prisoner in the Vigo County jail.

Upon his release, Tosser switched businesses by starting his own little burglary gang. They hit a number of homes and businesses in six cities around Terre Haute. The police tracked members of the gang to a farm west of West Terre Haute in 1931. One of his gang, Clell Lewis, owned the farm, and Tosser, his wife, Lewis and Hughie Peel were hiding from the cops. The police surrounded the farmhouse and ordered the gang to come out with their hands up. All but Bert raised their hands and surrendered. Tosser chose to jump out a back window in an attempt to evade the police. He had not gone far when a submachine gun burped. Tosser fell dead.

In the fall of 1928, Myrtle Miller's body was found in a ditch near New Castle, Indiana. It only took police two days to arrest a suspect, a small-time crook from Terre Haute named Charles "Blinky" Beasley. He got his nickname because he had a damaged eye that blinked with the regularity of a healthy heartbeat.

Arrested with Blinky was a woman named Irene Moyer and another hood named Harry Patterson. Each denied the charge, but Moyer soon gave in and offered several different versions of the murder after she was found. It took a while to root out the truth.

Blinky Beasley was a character on the fringe of the Terre Haute underworld. A little bootlegging and thieving were part of his repertoire. He did develop a specialty, albeit a minor one, as a shoplifter. It seemed an interesting choice for a hard case like Beasley. He had deserted from the army during World War I and spent a year at the military prison in Leavenworth. He was arrested in 1925 for clubbing an old man to death during a robbery in a Terre Haute alley. He was released due to a lack of evidence.

The plot that led to Myrtle Miller's death began in Moyer's Terre Haute home. Moyer, described as an "attractive Terre Haute flapper-wife," was estranged from her husband and seeing Patterson, another small-time crook. With them was Blinky Beasley. They talked about needing money to tide them over until the prime shoplifting holiday season. Beasley knew that Moyer was friends with Miller, whose brother lived in Terre Haute, and was known to have nice jewelry left from her divorce. According to

Moyer, Beasley suggested they go to Muncie to see Miller and ask her to go to Chicago on a shoplifting spree with them. Moyer called Miller, who agreed to go with them.

They drove to Muncie on Saturday, September 1, to pick up Miller. Moyer and Patterson were in the front seats, and Miller and Beasley were in the back. Miller was wearing her diamond jewelry. They drove around and stopped at a lover's lane, where Miller pulled a bottle of bootleg whiskey from her purse. The bottle was passed around as Beasley kissed and fondled Miller.

The group eventually left to buy sandwiches at a country barbecue stand. With darkness approaching, they drove on until Beasley told Patterson to pull off on a side road. Beasley reached under the seat and pulled out a revolver. The hand that had been fondling Miller now held the gun that smashed down on her skull. Patterson then completed the murder with a mechanic's hammer he had under the front seat. They dumped her body in a ditch along the road.

They returned to Terre Haute, where Beasley sold all of Miller's jewelry except for a diamond ring that Moyer kept for herself. Two days later, Terre Haute and Muncie police raided Moyer's house. In the process, Patterson

Irene Moyer and Charles "Blinky" Beasley during their trial for murdering Myrtle Miller. Muncie Star Press.

managed to escape, but Beasley and Moyer were captured. Police found Miller's ring in a paint can. It was clear they had the killers.

After being taken to Muncie, Beasley denied he killed Miller. He was a tough nut to crack, and the police despaired ever getting him to confess, so they focused on Moyer. When she realized she was going to be tried for murder, Moyer turned state's evidence and told the story of the murder. They allowed her mother to come from Terre Haute to comfort the frightened Moyer by sleeping in the cell next to her. Beasley, realizing that her evidence could send him to the electric chair, pleaded guilty in exchange for a life sentence.

Patterson fled to Chicago Heights, where he passed some forged checks. While there, he wrote a letter to the Muncie police denying he took part in the actual killing. Patterson was tracked down in Terre Haute. He was holed up in a "negro shack" when the police surrounded the house. As they rushed in, the police heard a gunshot. Patterson had committed suicide.

Up the Road

Roadhouses existed before Prohibition. They were usually set up in "wet" counties that bordered "dry" counties, so the thirsty just had to drive a few miles to get their booze.

But Prohibition made roadhouses a growth industry in Vigo County. In most cases, they were set up just outside the Terre Haute city limits. It was felt that their isolation out in the boonies made it more difficult for police to hamper business. They were sometimes set back along dirt roads behind trees or cornfields. There was also the hope that by falling in a murky area between jurisdictions, they would be safer.

And, of course, they were protected. One newspaper called them places of "gambling and booze; robbery and lewd women; fights and murders." They were protected by prosecutors and judges who adopted a "none of our business" attitude. After all, elections often depended on the support of the vice lords. True, there would be an occasional raid purely for show. Most of those raids came after arrangements were made that the roadhouse folks would get off with a fine or have the case thrown out of court due to "pre-arranged technicalities." Some of the raids were "ordered" by the bigger roadhouse owners to stifle competition. It was said that the roadhouses kept farmers in Otter Creek, the township north of Terre Haute, "terrorized."

Some were literally fly-by-night operations. A farmhouse by day would turn into a roadhouse at sundown. Word would get around, and customers would wend their way there for booze, gambling and girls.

But the most profitable were set up by longtime vice figures. Eddie Gosnell had the Oakview on the northern edge of Terre Haute. There were others, like Frenchie's, the Wisteria Gardens, the Bungalow and George and Em's on the south side.

The Bungalow was very popular. On any given evening (evenings in roadhouses usually ran from around 10:00 p.m. to 5:00 a.m.), twenty to forty couples could be found cavorting on its dance floor. They seemed to specialize in "vulgar and indecent" dances like the shimmy, the camel and the bear cat. The Bungalow, like many others, graciously offered their clientele private rooms for horizontal dancing after they became aroused by their sensual cavorting on the dance floor.

Wisteria Gardens was a little more sedate. It catered to a younger crowd. Frenchie's, where Eddie Gosnell was once a silent partner, could get particularly wild. In 1921, the Shriners held a convention in Terre Haute. One of the attendees was Archibald Dicks, a respected funeral director from Broadlands, Illinois. After a day of conventioneering and meetings, Dicks and a fellow Shriner were looking to blow off steam. In a time-honored tradition, they checked with a hotel desk clerk or taxi driver (taxi drivers were an essential marketing element for many vices and were often paid for each person they delivered) to find out where they might find a bit of relaxation. A taxi drove them to Frenchie's. Wearing their full Shriner regalia, they entered the roadhouse at exactly the wrong time. Conflicting reports were offered. The first was that Dicks was paying too much attention to someone's girlfriend and was shot. Another said that two "gangster types" were in a quarrel over the affections of a young woman that was settled when a gun was drawn and shots were fired. A stray bullet hit Dicks. His friend drove him to a Terre Haute hospital, but it was too late. Dicks was later buried in a ceremony provided by his own funeral home.

George and Em's, on the south side, offered a special depravity on Sabbath afternoons. It hosted cockfights and dogfights for the delectation of slack-jawed Hautean Neanderthals who enjoyed seeing "lesser beings" ripping each other to shreds.

Some came from near and far to sample roadhouse fare. In 1920, a doctor from Paris, Illinois, crossed the state line in search of some fun. He was "rolled" for $500, possibly after having knock-out drops slipped in his whiskey. He did not report it to police, rightfully assuming they would do nothing about it. Besides, he said, after showing his checkbook to a reporter, he could afford the loss.

A fondness for "white mule" drew a millionaire former Terre Hautean back to town from New York. He spent a wild week in the roadhouses of his old hometown. This was made clear when his checks started showing up at local banks. Despite living in the east, he maintained accounts at many Terre Haute banks. Enchanted by one "elegantly gowned, daintily powdered roadhouse lady," he gave her a check to buy her a new car. Her girlfriend was not to be shut out of that offer and said she sure could use a new car. She, too, was given a check, but as he was not as enamored of her as of her friend, it was for a lesser amount. But it was enough to buy her a "self-starting new Ford."

His little debauch became known when his checks, marked payable "to self or order," began to flood Terre Haute banks, which meant that some "queer characters unused to banking" showed up and were given cash for the checks. This may have led to alarmed bankers contacting the man's friends or family. A few days later, friends from New York appeared and took him back home.

He was greatly missed by his new roadhouse friends.

The Liquor Ring

Even though Joe Traum came to Terre Haute from St. Louis, he soon began to turn his eyes northward. He established a relationship with Al Capone. Over the years, the Chicago police connected Traum and some of his gunmen with kidnappings and killings in their city, including the legendary St. Valentine's Day Massacre. Traum must have been important to Capone, because Scarface gave orders to his mob that Traum was to be left alone.

During this time, the Egan Rats gang in St. Louis was on the decline. The gang that police once said was responsible for over one thousand crimes in 1924 alone was on the wane. Too many arrests had sent so many gang members to jail that it had left the gang in disarray. The Rats had also begun clashing with Capone. Two Rats gunmen, identified as St. Louis Italians, were gunned down in Chicago due to a bootleg war.

By 1925, Traum had formed his own independent gang. He was no longer beholden to St. Louis. Traum's bootlegging operation was working almost exclusively with Capone. This resulted in minor gang

THE INDIANAPOLIS STAR.
U. S. INDICTS LEADERS OF VIGO RUM RING

Terre Haute Liquor Ring headline. Indianapolis Star.

wars between Traum and his old gang back home that played out on the streets of Terre Haute.

This hardly pleased St. Louis. In May, a "bootleg squadron" from St. Louis invaded Terre Haute. Their job was to remind independent bootleggers they must buy their stock from St. Louis as always. They called a "bootleggers' convention," a sort of come-to-Jesus meeting to intimidate the attendees. A bootlegger from Taylorville refused their invitation. He was then kidnapped to force him to attend. The local bootleggers were told that if they did not go along with the plan, their shipments to and from Terre Haute would be hijacked, and they would go broke.

Traum did not appreciate encroachments into his turf. Additionally, the remnants of the St. Louis gang let it be known that Traum was a "weak sister" and no longer affiliated with them. That was fine with Traum. Traum would later use the "bootleggers' convention" tactic when he set out to create what would be called the largest liquor ring in the history of Indiana.

On a warm July evening in 1929, federal agents crept up on a farm in Burnett, just north of Terre Haute. They were expecting it to be just another night of axing a still. It was to be more than that.

They found five mash vats with 600-gallon capacity, two 1,200-gallon vats, a double still with a 500-gallon capacity and the most complete condensing unit they had ever seen. The equipment alone was estimated to be worth $30,000. Two men, George Aiduks and Joe Diaz, managed to get away through the woods, but John Barrelle and Ivan Mooney were handcuffed and taken away. That discovery would lead to the arrest of forty-six members of the Wabash Valley Liquor Ring covering Vigo and Vermillion Counties.

Joe Traum was the head and mastermind of the ring, which he put together in 1927. The ring had thirty-eight stills throughout the area. Not only were they making booze, more importantly, they were making corn syrup and selling it to bootleggers in Chicago Heights, Louisville, St. Louis and Cincinnati. Corn syrup, of course, was a vital ingredient in making booze. Just one of the "sugar walks," as these illegal sites were called, made over a quarter of a million dollars for the ring in a year.

Grand jury indictments were issued in 1930. They identified Joe Traum, John Jensen, Vigo County sheriff Ray Foncannon, gunman Ed O'Hare and Jack Bell as the ring's leaders.

Jensen, head of the Republican Party in Vigo County, was called the brains of the ring, but there was no doubt that Traum was the mastermind. Other important members of the ring included Dominic Gerino and Mario Bonacarsi of Clinton.

Bonacarsi was a grocer and wholesale feed and sugar dealer. The feds had caught two of his men driving trucks carrying two tons of corn syrup. Bonacarsi had supplied over three hundred tons of sugar for the ring. Gerino, who was said to be a representative of several steamship companies and an Italian consul, was the paymaster for Traum's ring. Forty-four of the forty-six indicted in the ring were either fined or sent to prison, including the Leavenworth and Atlanta federal penitentiaries. Even Jake Traum's wife, Pauline, was sentenced to thirty days in the Vigo County jail for selling liquor from her roadhouse.

More importantly, authorities said that four gangland murders resulted from Traum's ring—"Dutch" Rebec, Jack Morrison, Eddie Shannon and George Aiduks would not survive being associated with Joe Traum.

BLOOD ON THE STREETS

Sometimes, your worst nightmare does come true, or at least it did for George "Honey Boy" Evans. Evans was *the* power broker among the black community in Terre Haute. He also conducted one of the busiest gambling dens in Terre Haute in the basement of his saloon at Third and Cherry Streets. He was married to the infamous madam Lulu Brown. They were the king and queen of African American vice in Terre Haute. Evans was one of the most protected men in the city, because he controlled the black vote. While other gamblers were occasionally shut down or harassed by the police, Evans was safe, as no politician could afford to lose that bloc of black voters.

But Evans grew increasingly weary of life as a gambling kingpin. He confided to some friends that he was being tortured by ugly portents. He couldn't escape the feeling that his life would come to a violent end. After all, he had lived a life on the bitter fringes. He had made his share of enemies. Who knew when someone who felt he had cheated them at a gambling den would tire of thinking of revenge and finally act upon it?

Evans wanted out of the game, but he did not know if he could live without the money from gambling that filled his pockets. That was particularly true after Lulu Brown divorced him in 1919. She had demanded a $30,000 cut from his business as her settlement. He felt he had no choice but to go on with his vice operations.

One wonders if the hair on the back of Evans's neck stood up on that March day in 1920 when Albert Belay walked into the saloon. Belay was a black man from Evansville intent on playing a little poker. The game seemed to be going along peacefully enough until Belay thought Evans's cards were coming from somewhere other than the top of the deck. He argued with Evans, saying he was cheating. In a flash, Belay pulled a finely honed straight razor from his boot. One angry slash slit Honey Boy's throat so deep that Evans's head was nearly separated from his body. In that split second that the razor flashed, did George Evans have time to register that the fate he most dreaded was about to be visited upon him?

Another incident showed that until the bootlegger wars, gambling may have been the most dangerous profession in the West End.

Pleasant Cooksey was a "notorious colored gambler" and a clever one. When police tried to close down his den in a saloon, he moved and incorporated a new business, the Hotel Boys Club. He thought it gave him more respectability and was a way to evade new crackdowns on gambling. But his new venture did not insulate him from his past.

A black man named Nelson White carried a big grudge against Cooksey. It was the same old story. White felt that Cooksey had cheated him at cards. He lost a lot of money. But White did not just slink away and accept it as a lesson learned. Instead, he badgered Cooksey about getting his money back so much that Cooksey warned him that if he did not let it go, he would kill White.

White decided to strike first. Terre Haute held a street fair in October 1905. One of the main attractions was a Wild West show. It included shoot-em-ups and cowboys and Indians. Cooksey really wanted to see the show, so he left his gambling den to see what all the excitement was about. White saw his chance. With a pistol in his pocket, he snuck up behind the man he felt had fleeced him. He shot Cooksey in the back, killing him. The pocket muffled the gunshot, as did the guns firing in the Wild West show. No one knew anything about the killing until Cooksey crumpled on the street. White quietly walked back to work. When the police questioned him, he admitted that he had finally gotten his revenge on Cooksey.

Gang Wars

Gang warfare was inevitable. There was too much money to be made to not protect your turf. It was so valuable that war was fought foot by foot. Rides were taken. Assassins laid in wait in dark alleys. Machine guns spurted from

> **NEW GANG WARFARE SEEN AT TERRE HAUTE**
>
> Terre Haute, Ind., Dec. 29.—Gang warfare breaking out at intervals here in recent months today claimed its first victim since the shooting of William Highfield about one year ago, when William (Dutch) Rebec, alleged gangster, rumrunner and hijacker, was "taken for a ride" Wednesday night. His body was found today by the roadside west of Liggett.
> Rebec had been shot through the right jaw and his body dumped down an embankment into a small creek.

Gang wars. *Author's collection.*

fast cars. The streets of Terre Haute were not as bloody as those of Capone's Chicago, but more than a few red pools puddled on its sidewalks.

It was hard to know what to think of Floyd "Float" Haverstick, aka Float Washington, aka Floyd Washburn. He was lucky. He was unlucky. He was not the brightest fellow in gangland.

Haverstick was from the East St. Louis/Edwardsville, Illinois, area just across the Mississippi from St. Louis. He seemed to have a knack for getting into trouble. There was a warrant out for his arrest, likely for robbery. Well, Haverstick decided it would be a good idea to visit two friends in the Madison County jail in Edwardsville. Since it was not visiting time, he left his name with the jailer and said he would return the next day. Perhaps that was not his best idea. The jailer checked his name against the list of outstanding warrants. The next day, when he sauntered into the jail to visit his friends, he was promptly arrested. That little decision cost him some jail time.

Haverstick joined up with the St. Louis gang after his release, eventually running booze in and out of places like Terre Haute. In April 1924, he kidnapped and beat a Terre Haute bootlegger named Hagerman. He may have done so without permission from Joe Traum, because a week later, Haverstick was shot twice near Chrisman, Illinois. At first, police thought Traum was one of the shooters. That turned out not to be the case.

Haverstick was sent to the hospital in Paris, Illinois, to recover. His mother and sister came to look after him in the hospital. He told reporters he knew who had shot him. "I'll get Rebec when I get out of here. I don't want any action from the law. I'll do it myself."

During the last week of April, several men quietly walked into his room around 8:30 in the morning. They proceeded to wrench Haverstick from his bed and carry him to their car. Nurses told police that it seemed as if it was planned, as if Haverstick was waiting to be taken from his hospital room. They returned him to St. Louis. When the police went to his house, they found Haverstick hiding under his bed. They took him to a hospital and then to jail.

When he had recovered, he was taken to Terre Haute to testify against Rebec. He refused to identify Rebec, and the charges were dropped. Haverstick, Rebec and Joe Traum walked out of court as if they were best friends. Haverstick had been forgiven. He went back to running liquor, and other things, for Traum.

A rumrunner for the Chicago gang named Phillips was assigned to haul loads of liquor from Chicago to Louisville for the Kentucky Derby. He was not a lucky fellow. He was carrying 161 gallons of whiskey hidden in a secret compartment when the police caught him. As he was waiting in the Paris jail for the feds to claim him, he said this was his second unsuccessful run to Louisville. A few days earlier, his load of 160 gallons was hijacked by Joe Traum, Dutch Rebec and Float Haverstick!

Oddly, Haverstick and his brother were arrested in April 1927 for robbing two Traum gang members, including Tom Fagan, in Danville. They were released on bond but could not leave well enough alone. They waited for Fagan and his friend to leave jail and "curbed" them as they were getting into their car. In the scuffle that followed, Haverstick shot Fagan in the hand. The Haverstick brothers were immediately rearrested.

Once again, Haverstick was released on bail. He went back to East St. Louis and decided to do a little burgling. He was caught rifling in the basement of a local politician named Carter. When he tried to get away, Carter chased him and neatly placed a shotgun pellet just above Haverstick's left ear. It lodged in the right side of his brain.

In October 1926, the body of the "shot torn" William Highfield, one-time coal miner and father of two children, was found along a road north of Terre Haute. Highfield, a tall, handsome man, was a member of Traum's Egan Rats gang. Speculation was that he was another victim of a bootlegger war. Later, word spread that Highfield might not have died in Terre Haute but was killed somewhere else and had his body dumped in Terre Haute to create confusion.

Highfield and his partner, Dutch Rebec, learned an important lesson the hard way. You don't welsh on a deal. They were sent down to southern

Indiana to pick up a load of moonshine from a farmer who lived outside New Albany. The farmer had become a good supplier with the still he hid in a barn.

It all began well; the farmer met them and led them back to his farm. He helped them load the barrels into their car and stood back, waiting for payment. Perhaps Rebec and Highfield were a little short of funds and came up with the idea of hijacking the load and keeping the money they carried for the payment. The bosses back in Terre Haute didn't have to know that. So, when the farmer demanded his cash, they refused to fork it over. They drew their guns and told the moonshiner to step back. Still pointing their guns, they jumped into the car and turned it around.

Just when they thought they had gotten away with it, a figure appeared in a cornfield with a shotgun aimed at them. He told them to get out and drop their guns, but Highfield stupidly refused. Before he could have a second thought, shotgun shells tore into him. The farmers unloaded the whiskey as Highfield was dying. As soon as they had their moonshine, they told Rebec to get the hell out of their field and get back to Terre Haute.

Whichever story was true, Highfield was a victim of the bootlegging wars.

Homer Wright was a seasoned criminal who occasionally acted as Joe Traum's bodyguard. He was a bootlegger, hijacker, rumrunner and bank robber. He had narrowly avoided being sentenced as a habitual criminal, which would have meant a life sentence. The case was dropped when the judge discovered the police had searched his apartment without a proper warrant. He would play a feature—and deadly—role in two of the Liquor Ring murders.

In December 1928, Wright was staying at a house in Clinton. The house was being watched by some guys from St. Louis. His friend Eddie Shannon, aka Ewald Ukerle, had stopped by to visit his friend. Shannon left the house to walk to his car. He never made it. A car pulled up beside him, and the last thing Eddie Shannon heard was the gunfire that killed him. Oddly, Wright was arrested along with three others on suspicion of murdering Shannon. It was later determined that Wright was actually the intended victim in what was called war between bootlegging gangs. The gunmen, who did not know what Wright looked like, shot Shannon because he came out of a house where Wright was staying. They were heard to say they got the wrong guy as they sped away.

Wright's time came three years later. He was in Palmyra in southern Indiana when his body was found sprawled on a mailbox. He had either been trying to use the mailbox as a shield or had been tied to it while being tortured. A Terre Haute madam who had gone to school with Wright and known him all his life thought she knew why he was killed and who did it.

The feds had been tapping Wright's phone for over a year. The wiretaps gave them information about booze shipments that were then stopped and seized. Too often, they were shipments Wright had organized or been involved in. Joe Traum and others thought they were seeing a pattern. Why was it almost always Homer's shipments? They couldn't have a snitch in the gang.

Madam X was also sure she knew who murdered her old friend. She was well acquainted with Traum and his gang. They often drank and gambled in her husband's saloon and visited her brothel in the red-light district. After the murder of Wright, two of Traum's henchmen, Tom Fagan and "Crooked Neck" Crane, came into the saloon and asked to wash up. She told them they could but had to surrender their guns like always. They always did that when they were there, but they refused to hand them over this time, possibly because she could smell that they had been recently fired. Seeing the look in their eyes, she decided that maybe they could keep their guns this one time. She went to her grave believing Tom and Crooked Neck had killed Homer Wright.

Jackie Morrison was a good kid according to those who had known him a long time. He was also a hoodlum with a long history of robberies and other crimes. For instance, he teamed with the notorious Jack Bell to rob a mail truck in Terre Haute. Afterward, Morrison turned state's evidence and fingered Bell for the job. People weren't absolutely sure that Morrison was a snitch, but it sure looked like he was.

At about 7:00 p.m. on February 2, 1929, Morrison and Blackie Traum were walking out of an alley onto Wabash Avenue. They did not notice the man lurking in the darkness behind them. Four shots echoed through the alley, and Morrison fell to the sidewalk. The gunman and Traum sprinted in opposite directions. Morrison was still breathing when a crowd gathered, drawn by the gunfire. An ambulance was called, and Morrison was still conscious when he got to the hospital, where police interrogated him.

He knew who the gunman was, but he sure as hell wasn't going to tell the cops. Breathing shallowly, he said, "I don't want the man who shot me prosecuted. He was shooting at the other guy." He meant Blackie Traum was the target, but the slugs meant for him ripped through Morrison instead. He was probably right. Just a few days earlier, shots had been fired into Blackie Traum's bedroom. He and his wife were uninjured, because they had feared such an attack and moved into another room. Jackie Morrison died soon after he was shot.

A few years later, Morrison's wife, Margaret, was in trouble. To support herself (and possibly a drug habit), she became a drug dealer. She and her friend Katherine Murphy were returning from a drug-buying trip in Cleveland. They made the mistake of selling twenty-five dollars of drugs to an undercover federal agent. Word went out, and their car was stopped in Indiana. The police ordered them out of the car. As the police were discussing the arrest, the women jumped back in the car and sped off. One policeman jumped on the running board while his partner fired five shots into the moving vehicle. The women were arrested.

After George Aiduks was eventually captured for his part in the huge bootlegging operation in Burnett, he made the mistake of confessing to the crime and incriminating the Traums and others. While driving with a friend near downtown Terre Haute on September 6, 1929, he noticed a car following them. He tried to evade it by turning on several streets, but they caught up with him two blocks south of Wabash Avenue. A hail of submachine bullets ended Aiduks's pleasant drive and his life.

William "Dutch" Rebec was a bootlegger with a violent past. Among other things, he had shot Float Haverstick in the 1925 liquor quarrel. He had just missed being killed when gunmen killed Eddie Shannon instead of him. In September 1927, he had gotten into a brawl with another hood named Cliff Donham at the Terre Haute Traction Terminal. A large crowd saw the hand-to-hand combat that took place. Rebec's violent past caught up with him four days after Christmas in 1927.

Rebec was kidnapped and driven to the tiny hamlet of Liggett beyond West Terre Haute. Local farmers heard a car driving up and down country lanes as if they were looking for something. When they heard shots, they went back to sleep. Someone was always shooting at chicken thieves on the area farms.

Instead, it was shots being fired into Rebec's jaw. Those in the car finally found what they were looking for—a water-filled ditch in which to dump Rebec's body.

Thousands Die

The murder rate skyrocketed during Prohibition as gang wars broke out across the nation. Some estimates put gangland murders as high as four hundred per month in Chicago alone. But no gang killed as many Americans during Prohibition as the federal government did.

In an utterly bizarre decision, the government ordered manufacturers of industrial alcohol to add poisonous substances, like benzene and gasoline, to the alcohol. Millions of gallons of industrial alcohol were stolen by bootleggers each year. Someone in government came up with the murderous idea that by poisoning the alcohol, it would stop people from drinking illegal booze if it tasted bad or made them ill. New York City chief medical examiner Charles Norris called it "our national experiment in extermination." As bootleggers hired chemists to "renature" the alcohol, the government added new and different poisons.

Certainly, bootleggers adulterated alcohol that led to the deaths of many, but not as many as were caused by the federal government, which killed over ten thousand of its own citizens to save them from the moral decay of alcohol.

GOOD COP, BAD COP

Another pernicious outcome of Prohibition was the suborning of law enforcement. There was so much money being made by bootlegging (and the inability to enforce the idiotic law effectively) that sometimes good officers finally succumbed to corruption. Sheriff Ray Foncannon was one of those who joined the other side.

Foncannon was a veteran lawman. He was elected sheriff of Vigo County and took office in January 1925. After only about two weeks on the job, he became a local hero after a confrontation with a local hoodlum.

On Saturday, January 17, the sheriff's office received a call at around 2:00 in the afternoon. Someone from Fontanet, about ten miles from Terre Haute, was excitedly yelling that there was a riot going on and a gang was shooting up the town. Foncannon and three deputies jumped in a squad car and headed east on U.S. Highway 40. They did not know what they getting into or whose gang it was. They did not know they would be encountering a convicted killer who was not thought to be entirely sane.

Henry McDonald was involved in one of the most famous incidents in Terre Haute history. He was a minor hood who ran a "soft drink parlor" in Sanford, Indiana, northwest of town across the Wabash River. In 1908, his little operation was shut down because he was selling something harder than soda. In McDonald's fevered mind, the proper response was to dynamite a Big Four train as it passed through Sanford. That would teach them!

McDonald was fidgety during his trial. He didn't like police or being locked up in the Terre Haute jail, although he once came to the aid of a jailer who was attacked by three chicken thieves trying to get his keys and break out. On the day of the verdict, McDonald sat quietly awaiting word of his fate.

He was relieved when the jury foreman announced he was not guilty on the first count, but as the words "guilty on the second count" were read, McDonald pulled a gun from his pocket. Evidently, it was not a problem to sneak a gun into the Vigo County jail, and frisking prisoners was not high on the to-do list for jailers or those assigned to courthouse security.

Almost before the words were out of the foreman's mouth, McDonald started firing. Suddenly, all was madness as the sound of shouts and scraping chairs saturated the air. One of the first bullets exploded into the body of Detective William E. Dwyer. He lay bleeding as the courtroom filled with whizzing bullets. McDonald wounded Chief of Police Harvey Jones and two other officers before he was shot. Both McDonald and Dwyer were rushed to the hospital.

Disgraced Vigo County sheriff Ray Foncannon, 1930. *Author's collection.*

Dwyer was dead, and McDonald was hanging on but in serious condition. Fearing a mob forming to perhaps lynch McDonald, police kept him at the hospital.

When he recovered, McDonald was tried for first-degree murder. He pleaded not guilty by reason of insanity. After a long trial, he was convicted of manslaughter and sentenced to two to twenty-one years. He was sent to the criminally insane ward at the Indiana State Penitentiary at Michigan City. His sentence was commuted seven years later by Governor James Goodrich. When McDonald returned to Terre Haute, one of his first visits was to prosecutor James Cooper's office. The first bullet that McDonald fired in the courtroom in 1925 had been intended for Cooper, who narrowly escaped being hit. McDonald apologized for trying to kill Cooper and promised he would become a "good law-abiding citizen."

It was a promise he did not keep. Ten years later, he was running a blind tiger liquor joint in Fontanet.

Sheriff Foncannon and his deputies stopped into a store opposite McDonald's bootleg joint, asking about the reason for the riot call. An obviously nervous clerk told them everything was quiet and there had been no trouble. Foncannon did not believe him and entered another store looking for information. The reluctant witness there initially agreed that all was well but finally told them there had been fighting and threats of killings, but no shots had been fired. The trouble came from the gang in the blind tiger.

What happened next was breathlessly told by a reporter from the *Brazil Daily Times*. As his fevered account testifies, he must have been a Dashiell Hammett fan.

As Foncannon was questioning the store owner, McDonald surreptitiously entered the store, gun in hand. He asked if the sheriff was looking for him. Foncannon, who had never met McDonald or seen a poster of him, asked him who he was.

McDonald sneered and replied, "McDonald is my name, you damn son of a bitch. You get back in your machine out there and get out of this town. I'll kill you right now if you don't." McDonald pointed his gun at Foncannon's head.

Foncannon tried to stay calm. "Well, let's go outside and talk about this. You surely don't want to kill anybody, do you?"

"I don't give a god damn. There ain't nobody goin' to arrest me and I don't want no officers around here."

Foncannon turned to walk out the door. McDonald followed, his blue steel .38 revolver thrust into Foncannon's ribs. They went outside, where three deputies waited in the car. They had seen McDonald go into the store but had no idea that he was the troublemaker. Seeing the gun in the sheriff's ribs, they sat quietly. Foncannon opened the squad car door, which was a mistake. McDonald saw the riot guns and began screaming at the officers. "Where is Bill Hayes?"

Hoping to calm McDonald, Foncannon told McDonald he was sure he didn't want trouble. That set off McDonald again, who shouted he did not give a good god damn about any law and vowed that the "whole U.S. Army couldn't arrest me." While McDonald went on with his "I am the king of the world" rant, he had lowered the gun. It was now aimed at the ground, not at Foncannon.

According to the reporter, Foncannon twisted his shoulder sideways, opened his coat and unholstered his own .38. He shot McDonald before the killer could raise his own gun. Foncannon then dropped his gun and grabbed McDonald's gun hand while wrapping his right hand around McDonald's neck.

McDonald did not go easily. The two wrestled along the street. The deputies piled out of the car, guns in hand. But they could not shoot, fearing they might hit the sheriff as he and McDonald continued to twist and turn. As Foncannon punched McDonald, one of his deputies pushed his gun into the middle of the brawl. With his gun only a few inches from the sheriff's nose, the deputy fired, sending McDonald sprawling onto the dirt road. McDonald was dead within two minutes.

Upon hearing the shots, McDonald's gang, who had been watching from the blind tiger, rushed out and started for the wild scene. A few blasts into the air from the riot guns sent them scurrying away.

When word of the new sheriff's heroism spread, Foncannon was praised from the pulpits of Terre Haute churches. It was okay to kill, said the ministers, if it meant upholding the law.

Foncannon went on with his crime-busting. He took part in raids big and small. The next year, he shut down a barbecue joint called the White Rose that was serving more than ribs to its young clientele. Working with federal agents, he took part in shutting down a counterfeiting ring. Working with a local banker, they traced the source of the bogus bills both to Universal and Clinton, Indiana. During the raid, one of Foncannon's deputies found two suitcases bulging with phony twenty-dollar bills.

Foncannon also commanded a case that uncovered a scheme in which a local doctor received stolen goods from gangsters in exchange for taking care of any gang member wounded during robberies or gang wars. There had been about twenty robberies in Terre Haute, and some of the loot was recovered in a raid on Dr. R.J. Danner's office. Danner had an interesting past. In 1923, when he was a doctor in West Terre Haute, he had become involved with a patient. The patient's husband confronted him on West Terre Haute's main street with the intention of having it out with Danner. After taking a beating, Danner limped back to his office, picked up his pistol and returned to shoot the man. After the death of the aggrieved husband, Danner divorced his wife and married the woman whom he had made a widow.

Foncannon seemed like quite a bloodhound in tracking down bootleggers. He led raids that captured over one thousand bottles of home brew and thousands of gallons of liquor. That is why it was a surprise when he was found to have been walking on both sides of the street. Instead of working to close down a bootlegger gang called the Wabash Valley Liquor Ring, he was protecting them for a payoff. He would bust rival bootleggers and tip off the Wabash Valley gang led by Joe Traum about when the feds

Foncannon makes headlines. Indianapolis News.

planned to raid his operations. When Foncannon refused to cooperate with a federal investigation, he was cited for contempt in 1927. Authorities began looking into those claims and others that he gave special privileges to federal prisoners in his jail.

Just when Foncannon became corrupted is not known. Maybe he had been crooked all along. As a lawman, he had a long history with Terre Haute hoods like Buster Clark, Eddie Gosnell and the Traum brothers. Maybe he just got tired of seeing gangsters becoming rich, no matter how many times he arrested them. But he had sought and was paid protection money from the gangs.

Foncannon then became a part of a massive federal trial in Indianapolis.

Some interesting things came out during the investigation. Clark's sister Dot told of James Jensen forcing her and other gangsters' wives to contribute to the Republican campaign fund. She even went up and down the West End soliciting contributions from madams and the girls.

Clark testified that Jensen not only tipped him off to possible raids but when to cease his bootlegging while the heat was on. He resumed his activities when it seemed safe to do so.

Witnesses revealed that Foncannon was paid $500 per month in protection money by various bootleggers. Another bootlegger reported that the sheriff forced him to attend a "bootleggers' convention," where bootleggers were told they must by their booze from St. Louis via the Traum gang. It was alleged that the sheriff collaborated with the gangs by giving special privileges to the federal prisoners held in the Vigo County jail. Those prisoners included Buster Clark. Foncannon allowed them to smoke and play cards together in the jail basement. When he or his chief deputy were gone, they actually made one of the prisoners the turnkey. In essence, that turnkey could unlock any cell and let the prisoners roam. He even gave

Frank Meharry time out of jail to see his wife. During that visit, Meharry and his wife got into an argument that ended with Meharry beating her.

The court convicted Foncannon in 1930. He was given the heaviest sentence: eighteen months in prison and a $2,000 fine. In five years, Ray Foncannon had gone from lawman hero to Leavenworth prisoner No. 36895.

Foncannon was far from alone. Clinton police chief Wilmot Connors was convicted during the same trial, though he was given a much lighter sentence. Three Vigo County deputy sheriffs were convicted of protecting bootleggers. Richard Lidster, John Reese and George Storms were extorting protection money from two Terre Haute bootleggers. They also had the habit of keeping some of the liquor they seized in raids for themselves. They were given fifteen-month prison sentences and fined $500.

Forrest Marshall, who had been both a Terre Haute policeman and a deputy sheriff, found another way to help gangsters. In 1929, he stole a submachine gun from the Terre Haute National Guard Armory and sold it to Cliff Donham. Dennis Shea, who had been police chief under crooked mayor Donn Roberts and joined the mayor in Leavenworth, was arrested again in 1927. He was given six months and fined $500 for selling bootleg liquor and maintaining a common nuisance.

RED LIGHT, RED LIGHT

During World War I, young Hilda Hants was working nights as a "Hello Girl," an operator at the telephone company center on Wabash Avenue in Terre Haute. These were the days when all calls were operator-assisted, and she worked in front of one of those huge switchboards plugging in wires to connect calls.

This was one of those times when efforts were being made to close down the notorious brothels of the Hoosier state's sin city to protect the health and morals of soldiers and the citizenry (one wonders if they were sanguine about the efforts made by their more upright brethren to "protect" them). One night, the switchboard literally lit up and constantly buzzed. The fevered calls were from prostitutes and madams (conservative estimates put the number of prostitutes in the Terre Haute area at between seven hundred and one thousand at that time) to their local customers. Hants and a friend giddily listened in as they connected the local soiled doves to some of the most prominent and upright men in the city to finance their journeys to and stays in places like Chicago and Evansville. Sometimes, their cajoling turned into threats of exposure if the swains hesitated to come forward with the cash.

As they listened, Hants and her girlfriend conceived of the idea of going to the train station when their shift ended at midnight. This they did, likely flush with the guilty pleasure of it all. There, they watched skulking men surreptitiously slipping envelopes into the lacquered fingers of fashionably dressed women with painted faces.

The Reverend Mr. Keen

With its reputation, Terre Haute was made for Reverend Charles Keen. He might have said that the Lord sent him to Terre Haute to do his good work.

Keen arrived in Terre Haute in August 1907. He immediately went to the Volunteers of America office and, at their suggestion, the YMCA. Keen presented his credentials to H.E. Dodge, the head of the YMCA. He announced that he was a veteran of the slums of London, where he had done much good work for the Lord among the downtrodden. He wished to do the same in America, and he heard that Terre Haute was much in need of his service.

Keen handed Dodge a letter from the Baptist Mission Church of London. It was fulsome in its praise of Keen. "We sincerely recommend Brother Keen to our brethren across the sea.... He preaches the Divine Truth with power and force. He has proved himself to be...good godly Christian gentleman." Any church in America would count itself fortunate to have him.

Dodge was deeply impressed, particularly when Keen told him he would do a tour of Terre Haute's sinful areas and help Dodge rouse calls for reform by speaking publicly about what he found. Dodge introduced Keen to members of the Terre Haute Ministerial Association. They, too, were impressed and offered to set up a meeting at which Keen could enlighten all.

Keen set about touring the West End and other parts of the city, taking a city councilman and two reporters with him on some nights. He promised them he would find things even the "oldest inhabitants" would scarcely believe. His first report was given to the ministerial association meeting on Saturday. What he found shocked them.

Keen told them that he had observed gambling in saloons. At the Germania Hall, there was scandalous dancing known as ragging. There were ninety-five brothels in the West End, the red-light district. At least fourteen brothels were located outside of the red-light district. Even worse, there were 417 prostitutes in those brothels or scattered throughout the city. There were eleven unlicensed saloons, sixteen saloons that were open on Sunday and twelve gambling dens.

So shocked were the ministers that they did not think to ask how Keen knew the saloons were unlicensed or that sixteen saloons were open on Sunday when he did not tour on Sunday. Cynical newspaper reporters, however, were asking themselves those questions. Saturday evening editions began to question Keen and his numbers.

On Sunday, Keen spoke at the First Methodist Church. He spent a good portion of the meeting lambasting the *Terre Haute Tribune* and denying he was sensationalizing what he found.

He then told them the story of his life. He was born in a London slum, where his mother was nursed by a woman who had spent twenty years in prison. His childhood was spent among criminals, pimps and prostitutes. "I know criminals, all about them. I know bad women. I know saloonkeepers and I know many such persons in Terre Haute."

Hitting his stride, Keen thundered like a biblical patriarch. He saw many immoral women outside the West End. By 2:30 a.m., he had personally found these ladies of the evening out on the streets. He observed one house in which forty-seven men and women entered in three hours. He saw respectable young women accosted by "mashers" on the street. In short, conditions in Terre Haute were worse than any city of its size in the country.

But he did not stop there. He announced that there were twenty-two young women living in three houses very near the West End. What might happen to them with all the dissolute men roaming through the streets? And pawn shops! There were more pawn shops in Terre Haute than any other city its size. He saw a young woman go into a pawn shop and immediately "soak" the watch given to her by an admirer.

Continuing, he pulled out a blackboard and dramatically wrote "95" on it. He repeated much of what he had said the day before, pointing out that there were more prostitutes outside of the confines of the "district" than within the agreed-upon borders. He would supply locations and his findings in an affidavit.

The crowd was awed. Some of them pressed money into Keen's hands to aid his good works.

On Monday, Terre Haute mayor James Lyons called Keen into his office. Joining him were the chief of police and the prosecutor. Keen brought his slavish supporter H.E. Dodge with him. Dodge ceremoniously introduced Lyons to Keen and then asked for a private meeting with the mayor before proceeding. Lyons refused. Dodge asked that the chief and prosecutor be sent out of the room. Again, Lyons refused, saying everything should be public.

Lyons demanded to see the affidavits that Keen had given to the ministerial association. This time, Dodge refused, saying that the mayor had broken their agreement to a private meeting. Keen piped up, blustering that the ministerial association backed him. Dodge again pushed for a private meeting. Lyons stood firm.

Lyons then said he would have a judge subpoena Keen. He then led the pair to the police court judge's chambers. The judge ordered Keen to comply and be questioned by the prosecutor. Taking Keen through his public statements, he was able to point out all the errors Keen had made. Keen replied that perhaps the stenographer he used had made the mistakes. The prosecutor was able to refute most of Keen's allegations. The only concrete item Keen gave them were baseball pool tickets he had gotten from a saloon gambler. The judge ordered the police to arrest the gambler.

The judge then ordered that Keen be held overnight, as he was a non-resident, but bail was arranged, and the two very unhappy men left city hall. Lyons called Keen a "faker and swindler." The ministerial association issued a statement fully supporting Keen, and some began to speak of impeaching the mayor.

Keen eventually went back to the house where he was boarding. Around 9:00 p.m., he called Dodge to wish him good night. Dodge told him he would see him in the morning.

But Keen was gone by morning. When he did not show up for the 8:30 a.m. court appearance, Dodge went looking for him only to learn that Keen had skipped bail and departed the city. The owner of the house said that Keen had seemed nervous and inquired about railway timetables. He was gone before everyone got up that morning. Dodge wired London to seek confirmation of Keen's story. The ministerial association said they were "disappointed."

It was learned that Keen had sent two telegrams to Columbus, Ohio; he had told people his wife was staying there because she was ill. He told the Western Union manager to send the bill to the ministerial association. The telegrams had been sent to false addresses.

The Reverend Mr. Keen had skipped town, taking with him the trust of some in Terre Haute and their donations.

Word came back from London that they had never heard of Keen. The people of Terre Haute might be gullible, but they were not stupid. They knew they had been conned. They philosophically took it as "good riddance to bad rubbish." But they had not heard the last of Keen.

In January, word came from Kewanna, Indiana, that someone who fit Keen's description was preaching there. He had been hired to do a series of revival meetings. He was preaching as Charles Keene, not Keen. His topic for the meetings was "The Biggest Liar in the World."

By the time Terre Haute officials got word to the good people of Kewanna about Keene (or Keen), he had skipped town there, too, pocketing his fees for the meetings. Another Hoosier town had been duped. It seemed that Keen, "like the Irishman's flea," was hard to find.

Lo and behold, word came that Keen was under arrest in Denver. He had forged checks in Paducah, Kentucky, and defrauded a church in Nashville out of one hundred dollars.

Had the people of Terre Haute been more aware of theater history, Keen's name may have given them a clue to his purpose. He had adopted the name of one of the nineteenth century's greatest actors, an Englishman named Charles Kean.

The Business of Prostitution

Unlike gambling, which took money out of pockets in Terre Haute, prostitution was an economic driver for the city. It brought money into the city from visitors who patronized brothels.

As mentioned earlier, Terre Haute was a hot spot for sex tourism. One madam estimated that almost 90 percent of her customers were from outside the city. At any one time, she said, you could see numerous out-of-state cars parked throughout the West End. Some came in on trains or buses. All brought with them cash that was then spent around town.

When the area was temporarily shut down during World War I, no less an expert than Buster Clark estimated that the city was losing at least $75,000 per month during the closures. Calculated in modern terms, that equaled over $1 million.

Madams and prostitutes were good customers, and they usually paid in cash. The houses needed to be furnished, and that meant sales for furniture and department stores. Chairs, sofas, lighting, coffee tables, bedside tables and, of course, many, many beds were needed. These were purchased in downtown Terre Haute. Even if some did not change sheets after each "use," brothels needed vast amounts of linens. Most brothels did their own laundry, but others filled the baskets of local dry cleaners and laundries. Foods were purchased from local groceries, many of which made daily deliveries in the West End. Coal bins or oil tanks had to be delivered for heating.

But it was the money spent by madams and their staff that was the real boon to downtown Terre Haute merchants. As their income was higher than most women of the area, a visit from West End women filled many a cash register. They bought jewelry, furs, cars and many, many clothes. Madam X

Terre Haute prostitute, circa 1904. *Vigo County Historical Society.*

felt that the closing of the brothels in the 1960s and 1970s was a major factor in the decline of downtown Terre Haute.

The brothel staff did not have to go shopping to get what they needed. Future mayor Leland Larrison's family owned a drugstore. As a teenager, he would make two trips per week delivering cosmetics to fifteen or twenty brothels. While the average person could only afford to spend two dollars or so per week at the store, the West End women would spend ten to fifteen dollars per week—or more. Those purchases did a lot for the store's bottom line.

Benton Stein was a shy young man who worked in the family jewelry store on Wabash Avenue after school in the 1960s. Benton's grandfather and father would send him to the West End with a selection of fine jewelry. The awkward teenager would sit nervously while the women decided what they wanted from his stash. Some, recognizing his discomfort, would treat him like a younger brother, while others teased him to make him blush and squirm. Edward Massey delivered papers in the West End as a teenager. He always felt safe there. The women were kind to him, and they always paid right away for the papers. He did not have to return several times to collect from them as with other customers.

The Golden Age

Various dates have been given for the West End's golden age. Except for the brief crackdown during World War I, it was probably from 1910 to 1940. The brothels were side by side with gambling joints and saloons. The West End contracted a bit from its earlier sprawl. Initially, its rough boundaries were five blocks north and four blocks south of Wabash Avenue and from the Wabash River to Third Street on the west and east. Eventually it contracted to the area north of Wabash Avenue. It occasionally edged outward to the north and east, but in essence, it was between thirty-two and thirty-six square blocks that abounded with brothels, saloons and gambling dens. Every night was a carnival. The streets teemed with pleasure-seekers. Music and laughter spilled out into the streets.

Some brothels offered one-stop shopping for your vice of choice. You could gamble, drink, have sex or buy dope. Drugs were a much larger part of the scene than might be expected among both customers and working girls. Heroin use grew over the decades. Madam X noted that the houses staffed by addicted girls were considered the lowest end of brothels.

But the West End wasn't just vice dens. It was also a neighborhood. More than three thousand people lived within the district. There were families and businesses in the area, just as in other neighborhoods in the city. The farmers' market drew people from all over Terre Haute. A resident recalled his whole family going to the market on weekends to stock up on fresh vegetables and fruits. It contained a neighborhood grocery store, a dry cleaner and pawn and secondhand shops. It was just like all areas, except it was home to streets lined with brothels. A longtime resident said the brothels were just part of the neighborhood. When Prohibition ended, so did the threat of violence that sometimes hung over the district. And people felt safe there. "We never locked our doors at night," said a man who grew up in the neighborhood. Saloonkeepers and brothel owners knew order had to be maintained. As long as you did not cause any trouble, the police would leave you alone. In many ways, it was a form of self-policing by the vice crowd to ensure minimal interference by local authorities.

The West End was also a tourist attraction. Howard Batman, a longtime Terre Haute attorney and political figure, said he would often see cars from many other states slowly driving through the area. People would drive through with their heads thrust out the windows to catch a peek of the houses. Sometimes, there would be several women in a car ogling the women, pointing their fingers and giggling as they drove through during the daytime.

Edith Brown and her "girls," circa 1914. *Vigo County Historical Society*.

And the numbers? Many, many estimates have been posited over the years—some ridiculously high, like those of Reverend Charles Keen. So what was the high point of the golden age? It was likely between 1925 and 1935. Census records and city directories are helpful tools if you know the "code"—by comparing the addresses of known brothels with how they were designated, it is obvious that Terre Haute city directories listed brothel locations as "vacant" rather than giving their true status. The 1932 directory listed twenty-five "vacant" spots on three blocks along north Second Street, the epicenter of the red-light district. It is safe to say that at its busiest point, there were between fifty-five and sixty brothels housing between 850 and 1,000 prostitutes in the West End. And that is why Terre Haute became known as a "sin city."

A MADAM'S LIFE

The Special Collections Department of the Vigo County Public Library in Terre Haute holds an extraordinary recording—a two-and-a-half-hour oral history conducted in 1981 with a woman who was a madam of West End brothels. Many regarded her "houses" as second only to Madam Edith Brown's. The transcript of the recording is ninety-five pages long. It is an invaluable document for those researching prostitution and the social mores of the time. In the recording, she talks about her life and the world she inhabited. Because she did the interview with the stipulation that it be anonymous, she will be identified here, quite unoriginally, as Madam X.

Madam X ran West End brothels from 1925 until 1972, longer than any other madam. She wasn't there in the beginning, but she was there at the end. Hers was one of the final three houses shut down when the red-light district was closed forever by Terre Haute mayor Bill Brighton. She witnessed more life in that corner of sin city than anyone.

Madam X was born in St. Louis in 1902. After being sexually harassed by most of her bosses, she decided she'd had enough of that life. She wanted to be her own boss. She began by running a house of assignation, where she rented out rooms to streetwalkers so they had a place to bring their johns. It was a short step to becoming a true madam.

After passing through Terre Haute, she felt it would be an exciting place to live. The red-light district was a bit "cliquey." It did not greet newcomers with open arms, but that did not stop her. She was rebuffed by several people when she tried to rent a house to open her brothel. She was forced to rent a cottage outside the West End. The landlord kept intruding, so she started to look in the West End again. Finally, she found a place and opened her own brothel in 1925. Other madams tried to steer customers away from her or prevent her from getting the best girls. She persevered but felt it was another ten years before she was more or less accepted.

Even then, she had few friends among the madams except Edith Brown. Others thought her big-headed. She did not smoke, drink or carouse as most others did. She had a personal library that contained one thousand books. Over time, she became an acknowledged local expert on antiques. She was not your typical madam; perhaps that is why she lasted forty-seven years in the job. She knew what she was doing.

Staff Training

Part of a madam's job was to train her girls in the proper way to act and dress. Many were young country girls who were hardly refined. The best madams ran a sort of finishing school for prostitutes. In the better houses, like those of Madam X and Edith Brown, the women had to comport themselves as ladies. They weren't to use coarse language in front of customers or flaunt themselves in front of the clients. Though Madam Brown usually insisted her girls wear evening dress, others were more relaxed. Madam X was less strict with her dress code. Her girls could wear dresses, sheer lingerie and hose, or other attire meant to inspire the imaginations of men. But whatever they wore, it had to be clean and neat. Their makeup had to be well applied and not look "like a painted slut." The girls were required to shower each day before going on the "line."

Tricks of the Trade

Madam X was very protective of her girls, so over the years, she became adept at "reading" potential customers. She said 90 percent of the men were from out of town, so she seldom dealt with men she knew. She learned to quickly size up a man. An experienced madam could look at a man's clothing and demeanor and immediately tell if they had money. The majority of men were middle-aged. She learned early that young men in their twenties or younger were trouble. They would try to get in without enough money to pay for a "date," and they were unruly. She was particularly wary of college students, because officials at Indiana State University were always trying to shut down the West End.

The only time she was ever arrested was when one of her girls let in a group of Indiana State University students who raised hell, and the police had to be called.

World War II VD warning poster. *Library of Congress.*

Venereal disease and pregnancy were two major concerns in the houses. The girls were taught to look for cankers or lesions when a man stripped down. Men were required to either wash their genital area or let the woman do it. Even then, you could not be sure. That is why she made her girls go to the doctor for a blood test every week. If a john had given them something, they could start treatments immediately. Even some of the regulars that the madam knew and trusted could be a problem. Sometimes, when a girl's regular wanted something a bit different but did not want to hurt her feelings, he would go to another brothel. They just hoped he "didn't bring us something extra," meaning a sexually-transmitted infection, when he came back.

During most of her years as a madam, the girls did not use birth control. Condoms were available, of course, but very few men would wear them, as they felt it diminished the experience. She recommended the girls use Vaseline for what she thought was its carbolic properties; she followed the old country maxim that "if you grease an egg, it won't hatch." Still, some girls did get pregnant. Unlike some, Madam X allowed girls with babies to stay in the house, at least for a while. Some went for an abortion, which was fraught with great danger.

LOVE

Sometimes, customers got attached to certain girls and vice versa. A prominent businessman from Paris, Illinois, fell for one of Madam X's girls named Alice. Madam X was surprised, because there was nothing that special about Alice. She wasn't the prettiest or best built, just sort of average, but the man from Paris fell hard for her. He would always choose her when he came to the house. He began to see her on her days off. He spoiled her. He bought her I. Miller shoes, the best of the era. Alice was so thrilled that she paraded through the house showing off her expensive new shoes. He tried to give her anything she wanted, ranging from jewelry to new tires for her car.

He didn't know that Alice was in love with another, a "no-good man." Alice was sending him most of the money she made because he said he was building them a love nest in Muncie. Alice thought it was heaven until she went to Muncie and found there was no house—but her boyfriend had another woman on the string. That did not deter Alice. She would not give him up. The affair only ended when the man died.

Alice was devastated, but she still had her Paris businessman waiting for her in Terre Haute. He bought her a house in a nice residential neighborhood, and Alice filled it with her friends and hangers-on. It was quite a good time. And the Paris man was footing all the bills. Alice even brought members of her family from out of town to live with her. All was going her way until a stranger knocked on the door.

Alice let her in. The woman told Alice she was looking for the businessman. Alice said he was not at home but should be back soon. They sat making awkward conversation until her sugar daddy returned and saw Alice talking with his wife. The party was over. The wife had her husband declared incapable of handling his business and took over the purse strings. No more visits to Terre Haute for him.

Madam X noticed a pattern among her married customers around major holidays like Christmas and Easter. They would bring their wives downtown to shop for the holidays. In those days, few men enjoyed shopping with the family. So, they would drop them off downtown and say they were going to the cigar store or maybe to grab a beer while they shopped. As soon as the family was out of sight, they headed to the West End to treat themselves to a little gift. On at least one occasion, a married man did not make it back to pick up his wife.

An older man from Illinois came to Terre Haute to visit a doctor and get a shot. He went to Kate Adair's house in the afternoon. He picked out a girl, and she led him upstairs. As he sat on the bed untying his shoes, he gasped and lurched over. The prostitute turned and watched him fall. She shouted for help, and people came running. Someone checked his pulse and said he was dead. Panic set in for a moment, then it was decided to call the police. Knowing the situation, the police told them to call the undertaker. Someone explained the circumstances to the undertaker. He agreed to tell the wife that her husband suffered a heart attack while sitting in his car, and the police brought him straight to the mortuary.

Another man, a politician, was a regular visitor to the Moody Jones place. He came to Terre Haute on New Year's Day. He liked a particular little blonde named Irene who worked there. They were "engaged very busily" when he collapsed on top of her and died. He was a big man, so Irene had a difficult time pushing him off of her. Irene ran out of the house screaming, scared to death. Ambulances and police came. They took him out of the house and called his wife with the bad news. The newspapers said he died on the street on his way to a football game.

That story is the basis of a piece of West End lore that has been handed down through time. In this version, the man was the mayor of an Illinois city. The madam called the Terre Haute mayor, Wood Posey, who told her to get him dressed and take him to a dark corner of a parking lot and leave him there. All seemed well until his wife identified him at the morgue and wondered why he was perfectly attired but not wearing socks.

Besides odd circumstances like that, Madam X had to deal with the vagaries of politics. A new mayor might come in and make a brief show of cracking down a bit, but it usually went back to normal soon. It was all part of the game. There was a mayor, however, whom she absolutely despised. Vern McMillan is often thought of as a mayor who truly closed down the brothels. In fact, it was the federal government that shut down much of the West End during World War II, but McMillan liked to take credit for it.

Madam X considered him "The biggest hypocrite of all the mayors we ever had." While McMillan pretended that all the houses were shuttered for the duration, they were not. It was all supposed to be low-key so as to avoid drawing attention to them. McMillan not only let many houses reopen but allowed a madam named Joan Lee to go further than the norm in displaying her wares. Lee's girls sat in the windows on an enclosed porch and appeared to be nude as they wore only flesh-colored bras and panties. It caused quite a scene as both men and women went by to look at the "show." That kind of display was normally forbidden in the West End.

A Day in the Life

Madam X's business was conducted much as in all other brothels. She split earnings fifty-fifty with the girls. Out of her share, she paid for their room and board, laundry and housekeeping. Not all madams were that generous with their girls. Madam X had a woman working for her who once toiled in a brothel owned by Al Capone (or Al Brown, as he then called himself). Al, looking to squeeze every dollar he could, made his girls send their laundry or dry cleaning to a business he owned. They were charged more than someone who walked in off the street. He also charged them four times the going price for a quart of milk.

Like some others, Madam X had maids and a cook to look after the girls, though she insisted they pick up their rooms and not leave it to the maids. She had phones installed in each of their rooms. This was for their safety and to facilitate business. Customers paid for fifteen-minute segments with the girls, and the money was taken before they went upstairs. If the fifteen-minute men wanted a longer stay, the girl would call down and tell the madam. A maid was then sent to collect the money for the "overtime." They could also call for "room service" and request that drinks be sent up. The maids delivered the order and again collected the money. If a john got out of hand, the girls could ring down for help.

Madam X did indeed consider her house a home for her girls. She had more than one thousand women work for her over the years, including one from Europe. She liked to think of her girls as family. They would often spend time together listening to music, reading or sewing. She had very few rules. They had the run of the house. She expected them to shower and dress after they got up in the morning. Breakfast was at 10:00 a.m., but if they did not wish to eat then, they could fix their own meals, as they had free access to the refrigerator. She did have some rules for her women. They could not smoke—or even sit—on the porch. If they went out in a sleeveless dress, they had to cover it with a shawl or scarf. There was quite a bit of turnover among the girls. Some would go work at an out-of-town brothel for a break and then return. Her only request was they "come in like a lady and leave like a lady," meaning no sneaking off.

Her brothel was open around the clock. No matter what time a customer showed up, he was serviced. Things got slow around the holidays, but there was always one girl, usually with no family, "on call" at the house.

Caste System

There was a hierarchy among the houses in the West End. Madam X felt there were four levels of houses. Their standing depended upon the house itself, the amenities, the quality of the girls, the cleanliness of the house and the men they catered to. Most felt that her house was second only to Madam Brown's palace of pleasure. The others in their upper caste of houses belonged to Kate Adair and Jess Hartman.

Madam X's best house was at 214 Cherry Street. It was brick with a plate-glass double door that had been rescued from an old Terre Haute mansion. It had hardwood floors throughout. Downstairs included her library, music room and several small parlors where those who did not wish to be seen could make their choice in private. Upstairs were five bedrooms where the girls took their customers. Each bedroom was equipped with telephones. Her house was air conditioned and had full baths upstairs and downstairs.

Houses lower on the scale might be "bowl and pitcher" houses without baths or running water upstairs. They might be in dilapidated condition. They did not have amenities like air conditioning, phones or room service. The women working in those houses tended to not be as attractive, had drug or alcohol problems and/or had sexually-transmitted diseases. This meant they couldn't be choosy about the men they entertained or what they charged.

West End brothels were great barometers of the economy. Madam X could always tell if things were good or bad by her customers. In bad times, like during the Depression, business could be slow. She knew how bad it was when some regular customers came and said they were a little short and could not pay for the full treatment. Instead of a "full package," they might say they could only afford a basic, which usually meant only oral sex or masturbation. The Depression also forced many sex workers to do "more" for their money. This meant submitting to "kinky" requests from which they previously would have shied away.

Madam X witnessed most of the changes, all the different madams and girls and a huge assortment of men during her forty-seven years in the business. When the houses were shut by Mayor Bill Brighton in 1972, she was ready to retire. She had no qualms about the life she lived.

FROM TERRE HAUTE TO ETERNITY

The brothels, dives, bars and gambling joints of Terre Haute were widely known and often played host to the famous—or infamous. Gangsters like Al Capone and John Dillinger and their gangs were known to visit the pleasure spots of the city.

But there was one celebrity for whom Terre Haute was almost a second home in the 1950s. James Jones was perhaps the most celebrated novelist in the United States at the time. His masterful novel about the peacetime army, *From Here to Eternity*, had caused a sensation. The novel's frankness shocked many, and Jones's rough-hewn, pugnacious character fascinated even those who thought the work was obscene. When the book was turned into an award-winning movie with stars like Burt Lancaster, Montgomery Clift and Frank Sinatra, his stature only grew.

Jones, born and raised in Robinson, Illinois, was already familiar with Terre Haute before he wrote the book. Robinson was only about fifty miles from Terre Haute, and Jones began his visits to the city as a teenager. In fact, he may have contracted his first case of venereal disease in a Terre Haute brothel when he was only eighteen years old.

Jones joined the army in 1939 and was stationed in Hawaii. There, he was a regular visitor to the brothels catering to servicemen. His frank descriptions of those visits became one of the most shocking aspects of his book.

In 1951, Jones became a founding member, along with Lowney Handy and her husband, of the Handy Writers' Colony in Marshall, Illinois. The colony's guiding force was Lowney Handy (who was also Jones's lover), who tried to maintain an almost ascetic atmosphere. She expected her writers to maintain a strict schedule that included them copying the books of an author they admired (her peculiar theory about how to teach writing) before moving on to their own books. They also were required to help with construction of the colony and perform other chores.

But Handy also knew her varied group of young men needed to occasionally blow off some steam. The writers were allowed to leave the colony on certain weekends, and many of them raced the twenty miles to Terre Haute bars and brothels. Jones would roar off on his motorcycle or in his Buick to raise his own particular brand of hell in the West End. Jones explored Terre Haute, drinking it in as novelists do. Who knew when something he did or saw there would make it into his next novel?

Jones was an almost weekly visitor to a particular house and became friends with Madam X. They shared a love of antiques, and several times, Jones tried to buy some of her collection. She said he was not always a "bed customer." He loved to come to the house and just drink Coca-Cola and chat with her or the girls. It seemed to relax him.

She thought he was a down-to-earth guy, though she did notice that after one of his trips to Hollywood for the filming of *From Here to Eternity*, he began to "affect those tennis shoes and little tight (I call 'em jelly bean pants), you know, jeans." He told her she should read his new book, as she or her house might be in it. In one of his books, *Some Came Running*, he did mention the library she kept in her room.

John Bowers, another student at the Handy Writers' Colony, left a vivid description of one trip to Terre Haute in his book entitled, appropriately enough, *The Colony*. It was the custom of the veteran writers to initiate newcomers in the delights of a trip to Terre Haute. This particular time, Bowers and the others started out at the Marine Room bar at the Terre Haute House. After a few drinks at this upscale watering hole, they moved to a "subterranean working class bar" along Wabash Avenue. After fortifying themselves with a few more (and cheaper) drinks, they headed to the West End.

They ended up at a brothel on Cherry Street. They went to the back door, which was so sturdy that it would have been easier for the group to force their way into a bank than the cathouse. After pushing the buzzer, the group was met by a short, thin, unattractive women. She expertly eyed the group to see if they should be allowed entry. Finally, she recognized one of the group, saying "I remember you." They were invited inside.

They were first shown into a large bathroom before being allowed into the parlor, which Bowers thought looked like a doctor's office complete with old magazines—should they want to read while awaiting their appointment. The girls emerged from behind a doorway. On offer were four prospective temporary partners. The first was a "well-built brunette in a peek-a-boo harem outfit" looking for all the world like a desert princess awaiting her handsome sheik.

Next to her was a weary-looking older woman whose face told the story of her years as a prostitute. She was wearing a slit skirt and very high heels. Next was a redhead wearing a revealing silk bathrobe. Finally, there was a pretty young blonde with a bow in her hair.

The hard-looking woman asked if they were boys just off the farm looking for a little fun. One of the group told the women they were from the writers' colony and were friends of Jim Jones. The older woman said she had heard of it and liked Jones's book. "What was it, the naked and something or other?" She had confused Jones with Norman Mailer and his book *The Naked and the Dead*. They politely refrained from telling her she was talking about Norman Mailer's book, not Jim's. No sense in upsetting a potential good bed partner.

The older woman brushed back her hair in what she must have assumed was a seductive way and started the real proceedings by asking, "Who wants a date?"

Bowers quickly chose the quiet blonde, who led him back to a room. The room was clean, with a linoleum floor and a much-used pink bedspread covering a narrow bed. She stripped down to just her panties and bra. He handed her the five-dollar fee. The blonde dipped a washcloth into a bowl of sudsy water on the bedside table. She washed his genitals in a very impersonal, clinical manner as if she were a nurse giving a sponge bath to a patient.

She lounged on the bed, one leg provocatively cocked. She asked him how he wanted it. Bowers was not yet experienced enough to know to ask for a half and half, which was both oral and vaginal sex. Instead, he said he would like the usual. She smiled, knowing she would only have to do half the work for her fee. She removed her underwear and lay flat on her back and parted her legs. Bowers pulled an ancient condom from his wallet. She insisted she was clean and to not worry about protection, but he insisted. She just gave him a look.

Bowers climbed on top of her. It was rather impersonal, he thought, as if he were in some way detached from his thrusting body. He suddenly asked where she was from and learned she was a fellow Tennessean. When he asked the inevitable question about how she got on the game, she simply said that she sort of fell into it. Tired of the chatter, the blonde tersely asked if he was "going to come or take all night?" Time was money in her line of work.

As soon as he orgasmed, she was out of the bed in a flash. She washed herself and dressed again, leading him back to the parlor. The others in his group had already finished and were sitting back with smarmy grins on their satisfied faces. Not wanting the night to be over just yet, they went to another bar, ate shrimp and drank beer before leaving Terre Haute.

All in all, their experience in the West End was pretty typical of that shared by thousands of others over time.

Madam X did take issue with some of what Bowers wrote. She was unhappy with Bowers's depiction of the brothel. She knew the house upon which it was based. It was one operated by her friend Rose Moon. She felt that it made Rose's place look tawdry, particularly his description of the worn bedspread. Rose always kept a clean and neat house. But, as she noted, those writing about brothels usually depicted them as tawdry. "That's where their taste took them, but it wasn't really the norm."

Jones began work on *Some Came Running* while at the colony. His Terre Haute visits helped shape the novel. All those sites, people and events stayed in his mind. In some ways, Terre Haute was a character in the book. Several scenes took place there, as when the main characters go gambling in the Twelve Points area, which was where Eddie Gosnell had several gambling operations. He "transplanted" a Terre Haute bar called the Health Office to his fictional Parkman, Illinois, taking both the name and description of the place.

Terre Haute is mentioned over forty times in *Some Came Running*. Perhaps the key to how Jones viewed Terre Haute is the way he presents some Terre Hauteans. This is particularly evident when women from Terre Haute make appearances in Parkman, usually as girlfriends of characters in the book. They are usually described as pushy, brassy, rather hard women. They were portrayed as drunken, grasping sluts. Such was Jones's version of Terre Haute. But maybe that's where his taste took him.

ANY PUBLICITY IS GOOD PUBLICITY?

Terre Haute's reputation as a "sin city" was steadily spreading by the 1890s. Over the next six decades, Terre Haute and vice would become synonymous both in fiction and reportage.

One of the first articles was in the *Indianapolis News* on July 15, 1895. Under the headline "Prairie City Is Wide Open," the reporter recounted his trip to Indiana's "sportiest" city. He was specifically looking at gambling and whether saloons were adhering to the state's newly enacted Nicholson law, which set closing times for saloons.

He found that few people in "anything goes" Terre Haute wanted the law enforced. The reporter visited on the first day all the saloons in Terre Haute were supposedly closed. The front doors of the saloons were all locked, but a knowing rap on the back door vouchsafed entrance to all you could afford to drink.

One enterprising German baker had a solution for his thirsty customers. He owned a grocery and a saloon. He spent the day baking large loaves of bread that featured a secret ingredient—a half-pint of whiskey hidden inside. More Terre Haute males did the grocery shopping that day than at any other time.

One of the keys of the Nicholson law was that any place selling alcohol had to do so in plain sight with no obstructed views. It was as if Terre Haute had never heard of the law. Curtains, screens and blinds still hid activity in the saloons. The town was served by over 120 saloons, most of them ignoring restrictions on what hours they could be open. From there, the reporter decided to go in search of gambling.

Some of those he spoke to claimed that gambling was not a major problem and that any gambling was on the down-low. If that was so, the reporter seemed to find them quite easily. In one saloon/gambling den, he encountered a country boy who had lost "everything but his breath" in a poker game run by greedy men whose eyes grew as big as saucers when they saw a rube ambling into the bar.

The reporter did not have to leave the main street to find any type of games—poker, roulette, faro—he might wish to play. Barney Gregg's bar at Tenth and Main Streets was awash with gamblers. At least nine other gambling spots were strung along Main Street. Terre Haute was a city of scofflaws, it seemed.

National attention to the tawdry side of Terre Haute came in 1891 and 1910. The *National Police Gazette* (the *National Enquirer* of its day) and the *Chicago Tribune* both featured articles that focused on the prostitution and gambling that ran unchecked in the city on the Wabash. Similar articles would later appear in publications across the country.

Terre Haute's rather squalid reputation was also featured in fiction. James Jones's depiction of Terre Haute and its people in his 1958 novel *Some Came Running* was hardly a flattering one. The most outlandish story about Terre Haute appeared in a tawdry men's magazine called *True Danger* in 1963. The issue featured a sensational article entitled "The Teenage Torturers of Terre Haute." The torturers were teenage girls who were "wet-behind-the-ears" but gloried in home invasions during which they would torture the residents. The story was unbelievable, of course, but the editor likely thought that if such a thing was possible, it would be possible in a place like Terre Haute.

Three publications eventually led to some community leaders, who were not used to being heard, reaching a breaking point.

The first appeared in another men's magazine, *Stag*. Its November 1955 issue featured "Nighttime Girlies of Terre Haute," which the editor claimed was "an inside vice report." It focused on prostitution and gambling. There were prostitutes galore, its readers learned. They ranged from "high class house prostitutes, window-tapping line girls, blowsy hillbilly streetwalkers, cabaret pickups—Terre Haute's got 'em all." It showed photos of bar girls picking up customers (it was only implied that the photos were taken in Terre Haute).

Gambling was also on offer to anyone who wanted to find it. A bookie "line" took bets from all over the country. And you did not have to look far to find poker games, twenty-one or a spinning roulette wheel.

True Danger magazine with lurid fiction about Terre Haute. *Author's collection.*

The article caused a sensation. The issue sold out in Terre Haute by noon and sent eager readers scurrying to nearby towns to buy a copy. The magazine sold so quickly that some people travelled to nearby cities like Brazil. They didn't last long there, either. A newsstand owner reported that he could have sold a thousand more copies if they had been available. There were reports that some were so eager to read it that they paid two dollars for the twenty-five-cent magazine.

The outcry against the "dastardly, vicious, unfounded" story was immediate. Civic leaders stated that it was all untrue or a terrible exaggeration. The story was sensationalistic, as were all such magazines of *Stag*'s ilk, but many area residents had to acknowledge that some of it was true.

The article cost one Terre Hautean his job, and it wasn't the mayor or the police chief. Local TV anchorman Mike O'Neil was fired for daring to show the *Stag* cover on the air.

Much more damaging to the city's image were articles appearing in two widely circulated and respected magazines.

In the fall of 1956, Treasury agents burst through the door of a third-floor office just feet away from Seventh Street and Wabash Avenue, the "Crossroads of the Nation." They found six men taking bets over the phone lines. It was a pretty nice haul, the agents thought. Nothing special, but it was a good day's work. Only later did they find out that they had busted one of the biggest bookie operations outside of Las Vegas.

That story was told in the September 1, 1958 issue of *Life* magazine. The article, entitled "The Big, Big Bettors Hide, Hide and Hide," painted a dark picture of the city. The magazine viewed Terre Haute as a "thriving little cesspool of unabashed vice," a place where you could get anything you wanted for a price.

Why was one of the biggest bookie joints in the country situated in a grimy third-floor office in downtown Terre Haute? It was a case of one friend helping another. Joe Traum, a veteran hoodlum and "top gambler in Terre Haute," was friends with Leo Shaffer of Chicago. Shaffer was a bookie's bookie—in fact, his nickname was "Bookie." He loved making book, and the bettors loved the personable Shaffer. "Leo takes a nice order," said one satisfied customer.

Well, Shaffer told his friend Traum that he was looking for an out-of-the-way spot to set up a bookie operation. Traum, part owner of a Wabash Avenue restaurant named the Manor House, was more than glad to do a favor for a buddy. After all, he had an empty space next to the Manor House. Of course, his friend could use it. Soon, phone lines were connected, and "Bookie" was in business.

The quick lunch sausage hanging in a Terre Haute wire room for bookies to snack upon because they were too busy to eat meals. Life.

And business was good. Over $1.5 million in bets passed through the burning phone lines. The callers were heavy bettors from forty-three states, Canada and Cuba. So busy were the bookies at their phones that they often had no time to have a proper meal. They could not just leave their perches. Shaffer thoughtfully provided a six-pound sausage hanging from a string so the hungry could slice off a piece and take it back to their desks.

After all, they were taking bets from some of the wealthiest plungers in the nation. H.L. Hunt, millionaire oilman, liked to bet heavily on football. Four years later, he became a cofounder of the American Football League. Scientists and world-class bridge players also dialed Terre Haute. At least one celebrity was a regular. Zeppo Marx, the least talented of the Marx brothers, liked a bit of action. He, like others, tried to hide their faces (hence the article's title) when entering court. The worst blow for Marx was that his interrogation caused him to miss his brother Chico's wedding.

Mayor Ralph Tucker and other city officials were quick to point out that this was an out-of-town operation that was temporarily based in Terre Haute. That was true. Tucker, who liked a game of cards as much as the next guy, was unhappy that he was vaguely linked to the operation. His friend and campaign manager was friends with Traum. Tucker concluded that the article was published because it was a case of "Republicans always picking on Terre Haute."

Local gambling operations were not impacted by the big raid. They went on as usual.

The next blow to the city's reputation was thrown by the *Saturday Evening Post* on February 11, 1961. "Indiana's Delinquent City" was written by respected journalist and editor Peter Wyden (Peter's son Ron Wyden currently serves as a U.S. senator from Oregon). Once again, gambling and prostitution were the foci of the article. On his first day in town, Wyden came upon a roulette wheel in a club on Wabash Avenue. A few more steps took him to a bookie joint. There was no shortage of gambling joints in Terre Haute.

When Wyden asked Mayor Tucker about gambling, he was assured it was all small-time and private. He offered up an interesting metaphor to explain it. "It's like a woman walking around nude in her home without the shades drawn. You could arrest her for public indecency," he explained, "but what good would that do?"

And then there was the West End. Wyden noted that Terre Haute's red-light district was "one of a…dozen communities in the nation with a 'line'—a well-defined red-light district." Of course, prostitution was found in other areas of the city, but the West End was still the center for that type of activity. Some residents matter-of-factly told Wyden that there were only about a dozen brothels in town, as though that was a perfectly acceptable number—no big deal.

Wyden searched for answers as to why Terre Haute was as it was. He interviewed local community leaders like John Lamb, head of the chamber of commerce, and others. They complained the city was backward. There was no sewage treatment plant, no civic auditorium or public swimming pools. People didn't give a "hoot." Lamb deplored the deteriorating buildings and dirty streets. It was all due to a lack of will and effective leadership.

Little did he know that the article would spur a group of housewives to take charge of the situation. They would do what others had not. They would clean up Terre Haute.

AND SIN NO MORE

The *Life* and *Saturday Evening Post* articles were gut punches to Terre Haute. Many civic leaders fell back into the "it's not that bad" mantra that was their usual response. Everything that was written was "sensationalized"; they were always picking on poor old Terre Haute. But a group of housewives decided something had to be done. And if the men who ran the city were going to continue as before, then these women would have to take on the task of bettering Terre Haute themselves.

Four housewives decided to form a group to seek progressive change in 1961. They called themselves the "Housewife's Effort for Local Progress," or H.E.L.P. The movement took off immediately. They were soon joined by other women in town who were tired of waiting for change.

They published an open letter to Peter Wyden, writer of the *Saturday Evening Post* article. Unlike others who merely castigated Wyden, they took a different and more honest approach. They admitted that much of what he wrote was true. Terre Haute was indeed behind the times. The city had stagnated for much too long. New efforts and ideas were needed for the city to progress.

They also wisely chose not to just focus on prostitution and gambling. Instead, they zeroed in on what would later be called quality of life issues. The group pointed out that the city's infrastructure was pitiful. There was no public swimming pool, the sewage system was antiquated at best and open dumps were scattered around the city, breeding vermin and disease. There was a crying need for urban renewal via tearing down crumbling buildings. Ultimately, it would be urban renewal that led to the demise of the West End.

H.E.L.P. was not only fighting the physical conditions of Terre Haute but decades of corruption and indifference of the men who ran the city.

There had always been ineffective efforts to deal with prostitution and gambling. Each new mayor would take office and claim they were going to "crack down" on vice. The efforts worked sporadically, but the vices always came back. The only time there had been substantive—though short-lived—efforts made to lessen vice occurred when the state or federal government became involved, such as during the world wars.

Even though Terre Haute was home to one of the great progressive leaders of the United States (Socialist icon Eugene Debs was elected Terre Haute's city clerk in 1879), it was always a city of the status quo. One historian noted that Terre Haute did not "embrace many progressive reforms and [was] reluctant to dictate morals." That, and the fact that city politics were often driven by politicians whose only concern was reelection, held back the city. Though more and more people began to express desire for real change, it occurred at a glacial pace. The mayor in office during this latter period, Ralph Tucker, exemplified the status quo and "at least tolerated the old world free drinking males that continued to dominate Terre Haute politics."

Ralph Tucker grew up in poverty and spent much of his life in orphanages. He had an engaging personality that took him from salesman to radio personality to the mayor's office. He was "colorful" and had strong views about the powers of a mayor and the political machine's right to rule. His "mayor's car" was a flashy red Thunderbird. In this, he was much like Chicago mayor Richard J. Daley, who also served for over twenty years. Tucker served as mayor of Terre Haute from 1948 to 1968.

Tucker had a very pragmatic view of prostitution. Like many others before and after him, he saw prostitution as a fact of life, a necessary evil. The best that could be done was to restrict it to one area and maintain order within those boundaries. Thus, he had no real desire to meddle in the red-light district.

He viewed gambling much the same way. As long as it was in private and done willingly, it should be left alone. Tucker liked to play cards and bet on the horses. He was also quick on his feet. Once, while placing a bet in a bookie joint, he was utterly surprised when the place was raided by the state police, who rushed into the back room to arrest the gamblers. The mayor being arrested in a bookie joint while placing a bet would have done no good for his political career—or the reputation of Terre Haute. Tucker briskly stepped forward and announced he was the mayor and had been waiting there to help the police mop up the gamblers. He then ordered the bookies and fellow gamblers to line up and give the police their names.

Though Tucker's Democratic regime was known to take money from brothel owners and gamblers, he was generally portrayed as a man who personally did not take bribes. Madam X said in all the time he was mayor, he never asked her for protection money. At his death, the estate he left to his family was not one of a wealthy man. However, his personal bodyguard, a Terre Haute police detective, said that he would drive Tucker around the West End on Saturdays. While Tucker sat in the car, the detective would go to see the madam with a deck of cards in his hand. They would draw for high card, with the winner getting the agreed upon sum of money. It seemed Tucker never lost a hand.

Meanwhile, H.E.L.P's efforts started to reap benefits. Urban renewal began to take hold. Many of the sagging buildings in downtown were torn down, including some in the West End. A community swimming pool was opened in the largest city park. The sewage and water systems were gradually improving, though still inadequate. The often smoking, rancid dumps were being closed.

Ralph Tucker was succeeded by Leland Larrison. The new mayor, a Republican, was much different from Tucker. He was a dour, blunt man. He did share Tucker's view that prostitution was a necessary evil, and he had more important items on his agenda than brothels, such as getting a much needed railway overpass built.

Larrison, of course, was long familiar with madams and brothels from his days of making deliveries from his family's drugstore. He said there were only three "known" brothels and eighteen prostitutes when he took office in 1968, all of which could be seen from his office. Several madams came to his office soon after the election and asked him what was ahead for them during his administration. His reply heartened them. "All I want you to do is run them houses like it should be done. I don't want no trouble down there. I don't want any criticism on my part. If you run 'em right I don't think there'll be too much to it. And we'll continue."

They then asked him what percentage of their take he wanted for protection. He bluntly stated he wanted none. And he didn't want any Christmas "gifts" from them. Though he did accept some small things like an electric cigarette lighter. The madams left his office breathing easier than they had when they entered it.

Actually, it was Larrison and his chief of police who stirred up controversy about prostitution. A wire service report that one of his campaign promises was to eliminate prostitution and gambling in Terre Haute angered the mayor so much that he went on local television to deny he had ever made such a promise. It seemed an odd thing for a mayor to defend prostitution, but that was Terre Haute. The story caused *Time* magazine to take a closer look at the situation in Terre Haute in its February 21, 1969 issue. The report stated that "the mayor's firm stand in defense of vice raised a modest cheer from gamblers in the upstairs room at the Club Idaho on Hulman Street, and then they went back to their roulette and poker."

The reporter also mentioned the large sign on the door at Club Idaho that advised: "WHAT YOU SEE, WHAT YOU HEAR, WHEN YOU LEAVE, LEAVE IT HERE."

The article recalled the stories of Terre Haute's history of all-encompassing vice. However, there were some who were utterly shocked by Larrison's stance and his belief that prostitution should be legalized. Chief among them was Allen Rankin, then serving as president of Indiana State University (ISU). Rankin joined a long line of ISU presidents who had lobbied for the closure of the brothels since the 1880s. After all, "brand new high-rise dormitories [on the ISU campus] now stood across the street from battered old brownstones that housed the brothels."

Larrison snidely said he would close the brothels "if the college will get rid of the beatniks, kooks and hippies over there." Police Chief Glen Means decided to help out by tossing a filling station's worth of gasoline on the fire. He echoed the truism that prostitution was a necessary evil and that there had not been a single incident of rape reported in the previous year. Not satisfied with that, he went on to utter a sexist denigration of women and rape. "Oh, a few college girls hollered rape, but it really wasn't."

While the hoopla continued, Vigo County sheriff Clyde Lovellette raided three houses in the district and arrested nine women. The county court sentenced them to fifteen days in jail. Larrison worried that the six-foot-nine Lovellette, a former All American basketball player who led Kansas to an NCAA championship in 1952, followed by a long career in the NBA, was merely positioning himself to run against the mayor in the next Republican primary. The *Time* article was decried by some as another sensational broadside aimed at Terre Haute. Even ISU president Rankin, a critic of Larrison, wrote him a note saying that though he seldom agreed with him, he thought the article unfair.

End of an era. Terre Haute Tribune.

Larrison had a chance to close the West End for good but did not take the opportunity. When the urban renewal project was about to tear down the last of the red-light brothels, three madams, including Madam X, went to see Larrison. They said they wanted to stay together and continue to operate. He gave them permission to move a few blocks north on First Street. He agreed to this as long as they abided by the previous agreement and caused no trouble.

As a matter of fact, the number of brothels seemed to have increased threefold over Larrison's term. A new Democratic mayor, who took advantage of the changes wrought by urban renewal, turned out to be the one who ended more than a century of organized prostitution.

William Brighton succeeded Larrison as mayor in 1972. He made efforts to clean up Terre Haute's terrible image. Brighton took offense at Larrison's statement, aimed at Brighton, that "even if Jesus Christ were mayor and showed that he was, we'd still have a bad reputation." Brighton answered that "as long as we have a red-light district within two or three blocks from city hall and adjacent to a growing Indiana State University, it's impossible to put our best foot forward."

Saying that Terre Haute had ten to twelve brothels employing nearly one hundred prostitutes, Brighton ordered a major change that rang the death knell of prostitution in the city.

Previously, being convicted of prostitution meant that only a fine was imposed as a sentence. Brighton announced that prostitution would be prosecuted as a felony with a sentence of one to five years. Suddenly, madams and prostitutes faced hard jail time if they carried on as before. The mayor then flooded the area with police to enforce the policy. A few weeks later, he turned his attention to gambling. That, too, was closed down.

After more than 150 years of rampant prostitution and gambling, Terre Haute was no longer "sin city. "

EPILOGUE

Prostitution in Terre Haute did not just go away with the closing of the final three brothels. Some of the prostitutes may have gone to brothels elsewhere, but some just changed locations in the city. Instead of being focused on brothels and men coming to them, they had to go to bars or clubs to "pick up" customers. It became more of a "pimp-driven" business rather than "brothel-centric." There will always be prostitutes in Terre Haute, as there have been for over 175 years, but it is strictly small-time. The modern age is dominated by "escort services," adult websites and chat groups. A Vigo County sheriff's department official wrote that "there are the occasional 'out of town' pimps that may come in to town and bring a girl or two. Most of their business advertising is done on the Internet. None of which, that I know of, are very organized."

Terre Haute's "sex industry" shifted to adult bookstores, theaters and strip clubs. During the 1980s, there were up to six strip clubs operating throughout the city. There were perhaps the same number of adult bookstores and an adult theater during the time, but the advent of video and VHS tapes took their toll, and the bookstores and theaters are all but gone from the scene.

Miss Bunny Love backstage at the Idaho Club. *Vigo County Historical Society.*

Epilogue

Gambling held on longer than prostitution. There were still places, like the Idaho Club, where big gambling took place. The Idaho Club added "burlesque shows" to their menu before closing. One could go to see Miss Bunny Love do her stripper routine, then head to the back room to play some poker or roulette. The "Idaho" was perhaps the last vestige of Terre Haute's sin city until in closed in the 1980s.

There will be those who ask the inevitable question, "Why dredge up the past?" The author can only reply, "It is better to understand the past than to ignore it."

BIBLIOGRAPHY

Frail Sisterhood of the Bagnio

Clay County Enterprise (Brazil, IN). "Old Man Call." February 6, 1893.
Crumrin, Tim. "Sex on the Prairie/Lust at the Corner: Sexuality in the 19th Century." *Midwest Open Air Museums Magazine*, vol. XXV, no. 2 & 3 (2004): 15–25.
Daily Wabash Express (Terre Haute). "Court News." January 22, 1882.
———. "A Good Act." September 21, 1882.
———. "Jagged and in Jail." February 5, 1897.
———. "Suicidal Mania." February 2, 1883.
———. "War on Gallatin Street." February 10, 1882.
McCormick, Mike. *Terre Haute: Queen City of the Wabash*. Charleston, SC: Arcadia Publishing, 2005.
Saturday Evening Mail (Terre Haute). "A Lady Objects." May 26, 1883.
———. "Mrs. Volger." May 26, 1883.
Semi Weekly Express (Terre Haute). "All Were Fined." January 14, 1896.
———. "Ella Only Had $800." October 26, 1897.
———. "It'll Be Interesting." February 5, 1896.
———. "Looking for Gore." October 26, 1897.
———. "Raided a Vile Dive." March 5, 1897.
Weekly Express (Terre Haute). "Court News." May 29, 1867.
———. "The Murder." July 21, 1883.
Weekly Gazette (Terre Haute). "The Farm." August 16, 1883.
———. "Hard Crowd." July 26, 1883.
———. "In Her Favor." March 5, 1885.
———. "Just Sixteen." January 26, 1887.

BIBLIOGRAPHY

Curse of the White Queen of Chinatown

Batesville (IN) Tribune. "Opium Factory in Terre Haute." October 10, 1911.
Burlington (IA) Evening Gazette. "White Queen of Chinatown." May 2, 1901.
Terre Haute Semi-Weekly Express. "Opium Smoking." June 25, 1897.
———. "Paraphernalia to Enjoy Noxious Drug." June 25, 1897.
Terre Haute Tribune. "Dope Addict Tells of Thralldom." November 27, 1923.
———. "Explains How Dope Reaches the People." February 1, 1923.
———. "Local Drug Peddlers Strangely Protected." January 23, 1923.
———. "Terre Haute Alive with Dope Peddlers" January 28, 1923.

The Other West End

Crumrin, Timothy. *Til the Coal Train Hauled It Away: A Memoir of the Rise and Demise of a Small Town.* Bloomington, IN: Self-published, 2017.
Normal Advance. "People of the Dump." 1909.
Saturday Spectator. "Disinfectants to Be Applied to Taylorville." July 7, 1917.
———. "Our Squalid Tenements." July 13, 1912.
Terre Haute Sunday Tribune. "Station Is Open Today." February 15, 1903.

Duh Mayor

Evening Star (Franklin, IN). "Donn Roberts Is Released." October 28, 1918.
Fort Wayne Sentinel. "Donn Roberts Free and Joy Reigns in the Hut." October 24, 1918.
Indianapolis News. "Donn Roberts Rights Tuesday." September 3, 1936.
———. "Donn Roberts to Be Tried in Fall." May 23, 1934.
Saturday Spectator. "Former Mayor Said to Be Losing His Mind." June 12, 1915.

King of the Vice Trust

Hoosier State (Newport, IN). "Buster Clark Finally Convicted." July 7, 1920.
McCormick, Mike. *Terre Haute: Queen City of the Wabash.* Charleston, SC: Arcadia Publishing, 2005.
Saturday Spectator (Terre Haute). "Probe This Scandal and Probe It Deep." July 21, 1917.
———. "Slot Machine Gambler! There Is Hope." July 28, 1917.
Terre Haute Tribune. "Slot Machines Get Fines for Owners." February 27, 1917.

BIBLIOGRAPHY

The Queen and Crown Prince of Vice

Anonymous. *Prostitution–Terre Haute*, 1981. Vigo County Oral History Project, Special Collections/Archives, Vigo County Public Library. Terre Haute, IN.

Bob Ferguson, interviewed by Tim Crumrin, February 12, 2018.

Saturday Spectator. "Eddie Gosnell: Madame Brown's Husband." July 9, 1979.

———. "Government Again Come to Aid of Terre Haute." July 3, 1920.

A Gangster Named Boobie

Beineke, John A. *Hoosier Public Enemy: A Life of John Dillinger*. Indianapolis: Indiana Historical Society Press, 2014.

Crumrin, Timothy. *Til the Coal Train Hauled It Away: A Memoir of the Rise and Demise of a Small Town*. Bloomington, IN: Self-published, 2017.

Dillinger Gang Collection. Indiana Archives and Records Administration, Indianapolis.

Hammond Times. "Ed Shouse Will Testify Against Russell Clark." March 22, 1934.

———. "Estill Says They're Smart Gangsters." January 29, 1934.

http://www.dillingerswomen.com/Opal-Long.html.

McCormick, Mike. *Terre Haute: Queen City of the Wabash*. Charleston, SC: Arcadia Publishing, 2005.

Russell Clark Files. Indiana Archives and Records Administration, Indianapolis.

Yuma Sun. "J. Dillinger Captured in Police Raid." January 26, 1934.

Our Gangs

Blum, Deborah. "The Chemist's War." *Slate*. February 19, 2010. https://slate.com/technology/2010/02/the-little-told-story-of-how-the-u-s-government-poisoned-alcohol-during-prohibition.html.

Brazil Daily Times. "Barber Rushed to Vigo Jail." May 4, 1924.

Eileen Ellingsworth, interview with Tim Crumrin, June 26, 2016.

Indianapolis News. "Buzzards Must Quit Terre Haute." January 2, 1922.

———. "Rum Cargoes Seized, Gangsters Arrested." March 16, 1925.

Indianapolis Star. "Authorities Check Actions of Alleged St. Louis Gangsters." September 6, 1928.

———. "Liquor Ring Case Near Last Stage." June 14, 1930.

Journal Gazette (Mattoon, IL). "Accused Gangster Is Ready to Give Bond." April 9, 1925.

Logansport Press. "Awaiting Trial on Charge of Bank Robbery." December 12, 1924.

McCormick, Mike. *Terre Haute: Queen City of the Wabash*. Charleston, SC: Arcadia Publishing, 2005.

BIBLIOGRAPHY

Muncie Evening Press. "Fires Death Shot as Cops Enter Shack." November 11, 1928.
Star Press (Muncie, IN). "Terre Haute Raids Net Big Haul." June 30, 1927.
———. "Woman in Hiding Two Years Under Arrest." May 30, 1925.

Blood on the Streets

Anonymous. *Prostitution–Terre Haute*, 1981. Vigo County Oral History Project, Special Collections/Archives, Vigo County Public Library. Terre Haute, IN.
Daily Chronicle (DeKalb, IL). "Mystery Case in this State May Be Murder." September 15, 1927.
Daily Independent (Murphysboro, IL). "Haverstick Condition Critical." August, 17, 1927.
Edwardsville Intelligencer. "Walked Into Jail." March 7, 1924.
McCormick, Mike. *Terre Haute: Queen City of the Wabash.* Charleston, SC: Arcadia Publishing, 2005.
Terre Haute Tribune-Star. "Gangster 'Handsome Jack' Morrison Was Gunned Down During Prohibition." January 28, 2001.
———. "The Gang-Style Slaying of George Aiduks." January 21, 2001.

Good Cop, Bad Cop

Brazil Daily Times. "Henry McDonald Bites the Dust." January 19, 1925.
Indianapolis News. "Barbecue Joint Closed Down." August 12, 1927.
Indianapolis Star. "Liquor Ring Case Near Last Stage." June 14, 1930.
———. "Reports to US Court Charges He Freed Prisoners." June 10, 1927.

Red Light, Red Light

Anonymous. *Prostitution–Terre Haute*, 1981. Vigo County Oral History Project, Special Collections/Archives, Vigo County Public Library. Terre Haute, IN.
Batman, Howard. Vigo County Oral History Project, Special Collections/Archives, Vigo County Public Library. Terre Haute, IN.
Kadel, Robert. Vigo County Oral History Project, Special Collections/Archives, Vigo County Public Library. Terre Haute, IN.
McCormick, Mike. *Terre Haute: Queen City of the Wabash.* Charleston, SC: Arcadia Publishing, 2005.
Nasser, Paul. Vigo County Oral History Project, Special Collections/Archives, Vigo County Public Library. Terre Haute, IN.
Terre Haute Morning Star. "Keen Leads Party Through Red-light." August 18, 1907.

BIBLIOGRAPHY

———. "Mayor Calls Evangelist Keen Hypocrite and Scoundrel." August 20, 1907.
Terre Haute Tribune-Star. "Terre Haute's Red-light District Reopens in 1917." February 24, 2002.
———. "Terre Haute's Red-light District Was No Secret." July 20, 2001.

A Madam's Life

Anonymous. *Prostitution–Terre Haute*, 1981. Vigo County Oral History Project, Special Collections/Archives, Vigo County Public Library. Terre Haute, IN.

From Terre Haute to Eternity

Anonymous. *Prostitution–Terre Haute*, 1981. Vigo County Oral History Project, Special Collections/Archives, Vigo County Public Library. Terre Haute, IN.
Bowers, John. *The Colony*. New York: Dutton, 1971.
Hendrick, George, Helen Howe and Don Sackrider. *James Jones and the Handy Writers' Colony*. Carbondale: Southern Illinois University Press, 2001.

Any Publicity Is Good Publicity?

Anonymous. *Prostitution–Terre Haute*, 1981. Vigo County Oral History Project, Special Collections/Archives, Vigo County Public Library. Terre Haute, IN.
Indianapolis Star. "Prairie City Is Wide Open." July 15, 1895.
Larrison, Leland. Vigo County Oral History Project, Special Collections/Archives, Vigo County Public Library. Terre Haute, IN.
Life. "The Big, Big Bettors Hide, Hide and Hide." September 1, 1957.
Spann, Edward. *Ralph Tucker of Terre Haute: A Mayor and His City, 1938–1977*. Terre Haute, IN: Self-published, 1998.
Stag Magazine. "Night-Time Girls of Terre Haute." November 1955.
TIME. "Open House in Terre Haute." April 21, 1969.
True Danger. "Teenage Torturers of Terre Haute." February 1963.
Wyden, Peter. "Indiana's Delinquent City." *Saturday Evening Post*, February 11, 1961.

And Sin No More

Bergstrom, Laura. "Hautian Houses of Ill-Fame: A Midwestern City's Confrontation With Vice, 1910–1972." Unpublished master's thesis, Indiana State University, 2003.
H.E.L.P. Collection, Vigo County Public Library Archives. Terre Haute, IN.

Bibliography

Larrison, Leland. Vigo County Oral History Project, Special Collections/Archives, Vigo County Public Library. Terre Haute, IN.

Spann, Edward. *Ralph Tucker of Terre Haute: A Mayor and His City, 1938–1977*. Terre Haute, IN: Self-published, 1998.

Terre Haute Tribune. "Vice Lid Is On—Brighton." January 11, 1972.

ABOUT THE AUTHOR

Tim Crumrin is an award-winning historian and author. He received the prestigious Eli Lilly Lifetime Achievement Award from the Indiana Historical Society in 2014 for his distinguished contributions to history.

He holds degrees in history from Indiana State University and served for twenty-five years as historian at Conner Prairie Museum in Fishers, Indiana. While growing up in the Terre Haute area, he was fascinated by tales of the city's colorful past.

His most recent works—*A Sky Held Captive*, a collection of short fiction and poetry; and *Til the Coal Train Hauled It Away: A Memoir of the Rise and Demise of a Small Town*—were published in 2017.

He lives in Terre Haute with his wife, Robin; daughter, Brynn; and four dogs who graciously allow him to share their office.

Visit us at
www.historypress.com

www.ingramcontent.com/pod-product-compliance
Lightning Source LLC
Chambersburg PA
CBHW042141160426
43201CB00021B/2358